"Ram Charan spots the issue managers care about most—then shows them how to conquer it and win." —Geoff Colvin, *Fortune*

"Ram Charan has done it again! No one brings more business savvy and practical advice for turning ideas into action and desired results than Mr. Charan. Every day is Monday morning for profitable growth. Monday morning starts today—A MUST READ!"
—Doug Green, partner in charge, Leadership Development, KPMG, LLP

"Here is the book CEOs have been waiting for: a fresh reconceptualization of what sustainable growth looks like in today's hyper-competitive world and a practical 'how-to' program for achieving it. Ram Charan is one of the keenest minds on the global business scene. In this book, he draws once again on his uniquely broad and deep wealth of experience."
—William T. Solomon, chairman, Austin Industries

"The most telling insight ever written about how to grow revenues and why organizations fail to do it. This is the book Ram always promised to write and it is his best book ever."
—Tom Curley, former president and publisher of *USA Today*

"Ram makes it clear that growth is a constantly achievable result for an organization that is properly focused and empowered. He reminds us that our job is to provide the organization with the vision and confidence to deliver it." —Gary Mulloy, chairman and CEO of ADVO

"In our unstable world of today, achieving sustainable and profitable revenue growth is not easy. Bringing it down to earth with your own practical set of relevant and actionable priorities is hard work. This is where Ram helps to focus. And it pays off: improved bottom line and energy, personal growth for the people involved, creating value for your company."
—Michael Wisbrun, executive vice president,
KLM Cargo, KLM Royal Dutch Airlines

"In maximizing long-term shareholder return, consistent earnings and dividend growth, as well as revenue growth, are mandated by investors. If earning growth is simply based on improving expense productivity, investors question and discount the sustainability of future earnings growth. Investors demand and reward profitable revenue growth. In *Profitable Growth Is Everyone's Business*, Ram Charan clearly articulates the competitive advantages that can be achieved with 'good growth.' Successfully executing the ten tools detailed in the book, differentiable value can be effectively delivered to both clients and shareholders."

—Edward J. Brown III, chairman and CEO,
Banc of America Securities, LLC

"Ram reorients thinking about growth to small day-to-day changes. His focus on collaboration with customers is critical to growth. The implementation guide is practical."

—Chad Holliday, chairman and CEO of DuPont

"This book brings you back to reality, and at the same time gives you hope. It is practical advice that shows how much control you have over the growth of your business. It is in the consistency of day-to-day execution that you build the backbone of a great company."

—Maria Luisa Ferre Rangel, president and CEO
of El Nuevo Dia, San Juan, Puerto Rico

"Achievement of profitable growth is now attainable for everyone who follows the practical advice of Dr. Ram Charan. Putting this book into the hands of leaders throughout an organization will make profitable, organic, and sustainable growth become everyone's business . . . a prerequisite to building shareholder value."

—Jim Keyes, president and CEO, 7-Eleven, Inc.

"In bringing the importance of execution to the forefront, Ram's insight and knowledge have become invaluable for the global business community. This book expands on his management principles for profitable growth and reinforces Ram's position as a leading thought leader for business in the 21st century."　　　　　　　　　—Jack Mollen, senior vice president, Human Resources, EMC Corporation

"In an industry where 3 to 5 percent growth is top quartile, we are always looking for creative ways to get the most from our existing assets, while also looking for the next big growth area. In *Profitable Growth Is Everyone's Business,* Ram Charan outlines a number of internal and external obstacles to growth, then shows managers at all levels how to overcome these obstacles and create profitable growth in their businesses. He points out the importance of hitting 'singles and doubles,' creating a continuous improvement mind-set throughout your organization, and maintaining a disciplined and accountable approach to growth. This book will provide valuable insight to any manager committed to profitable growth."
—J. J. Mulva, president and CEO, ConocoPhillips

"A growth agenda is on the top of every CEO's mind . . . and Ram's simple but on-the-mark tools for building a company-wide 'growth culture' are invaluable."　　　　　—Joseph M. Tucci, president and CEO, EMC Corporation

PROFITABLE
GROWTH

IS EVERYONE'S
BUSINESS

10 TOOLS YOU CAN USE MONDAY MORNING

RAM CHARAN

CROWN
BUSINESS
NEW YORK

Published by Crown Business, New York, New York.
Member of the Crown Publishing Group, a division of Random House, Inc.
www.crownpublishing.com

CROWN BUSINESS is a trademark and the Rising Sun colophon is a registered trademark of Random House, Inc.

Printed in the United States of America

Design by Leonard Henderson

Library of Congress Cataloging-in-Publication Data
Charan, Ram.
Profitable growth is everyone's business : 10 tools you can use Monday morning /
Ram Charan.—1st ed.
1. Organizational behavior.   2. Industrial analysis.   3. Strategy.
4. Success in business.   5. Marketing.   6. Execution.   I. Title.
HD58.9.C485 2004
658.4'063—dc22
2003017654

ISBN 1-4000-5152-5

10   9   8   7   6   5   4   3   2   1

First Edition

Dedicated to the hearts and souls of the joint family
of twelve siblings and cousins living under one roof
for fifty years, whose personal sacrifices
made my formal education possible.

ACKNOWLEDGMENTS

Paul B. Brown has been a very effective collaborator in working with me to create *Profitable Growth Is Everyone's Business*. Not only is Paul a pleasure to work with, but the discipline and speed with which he worked, his sense of the reader, and the creativity he brought to the manuscript added significant value from the time we first discussed the idea until the manuscript was put to bed. His attitude was totally positive throughout, and his ever-present and continuing commitment to getting things right has made this a very productive partnership.

This book is as far from a theoretical exercise as you can get. It is based on what is happening in the real world. And the only way it was possible for me to really learn what was going on was for executives and managers at all levels of the organizations profiled in this book—and the ones only referred to in passing, or those whose identities I disguised at their request—to let me inside and discuss candidly with me the problems and opportunities they face. I appreciate the access and the time more than they will ever know.

My interest in business in general, and profitable growth in particular, can be traced back to my family's shoe business in India. It was nurtured and developed during my time with Australian Gas and Light and the Honolulu Gas Company, and then fueled by my work over the last forty years with clients too numerous to possibly mention by name. But although I don't have the space to list your name and affiliation, please know you have my sincerest gratitude.

I would also like to thank my many friends who spared the time—often on extremely short notice—to read what I had written and make valuable contributions.

John Joyce, my roommate back in our days at the Harvard Business School, has been a true partner, as well as a true friend, for the last forty years. He spent countless hours reviewing the content of this book and keeping me headed in the right direction.

In Dallas, Cynthia Burr, Heather Liebbe, and Carol Davis not only coordinated the hundreds of tasks that need to be completed in order to write a book, but they did it with remarkable high energy, efficiency, and good humor.

As for the actual creation of the book itself, the input from Geri Willigan, who has worked with me for the last ten years on my writing projects, was invaluable. She actively participated in the journey that led to *Profitable Growth Is Everyone's Business*. Larry Yu needs special thanks as well, as does Crown assistant editor Shana Drehs. Her constant, cheerful support and help made this project far easier.

John Mahaney, the executive editor of Crown Business, was a central player in the creation of this book. He understands what the reader needs. This thoroughly dedicated professional is the editor's editor. He was more than a partner on this project; he was also a coach, always available to make each version of this book better. He is the best of the best.

CONTENTS

Contents

PROFITABLE GROWTH
IS EVERYONE'S BUSINESS

Introduction

HOW TO GET MORE OUT OF WHAT

YOU ALREADY HAVE

PROFITABLE GROWTH IS EVERYONE'S BUSINESS is based on living research. For the past twenty-five years I have, on a daily basis, been observing what is happening—what is working and what isn't—while it is actually happening in companies around the world.

My experiences with many of these companies have been long term—a decade or more in many cases—and the ideas I have developed for solving the growth dilemma are based on personally seeing what works in real time.

These are ideas tested across industries and that deliver results. My goal has always been to improve the practice of business by giving people tools they can put to use immediately, on Monday morning, if you will. These tools can seem like common sense, but all too often the biggest challenge in business is the translation of ideas into action. This is especially true when it comes to obtaining consistent revenue growth. The ultimate purpose of *Profitable Growth Is Everyone's Business* is to provide the tools for people in every industry concerned about the prospect of generating sustained, internally generated top-line growth.* Many people feel that their base business is being eroded by such factors as the lack of pricing power, excess capacity (too many suppliers chasing too few customers), and global competition. They are also seeing that cost-cutting and productivity improvements alone will not be enough to generate the kind of performance that will satisfy either shareholders, or, more important, the employees whose prospects depend on revenue growth generating future career opportunities. And, eventually, lack of growth makes a business uncompetitive in the eyes of customers, since without sustained revenue growth, the ability to innovate declines and a company goes into a death spiral.

Many people equate growth with—in the language of baseball—"swinging for the fences," home runs that capture huge sales increases that will dramatically increase the size of their business. Growth is too often thought of only in big-dollar terms, breakthroughs such as the creation of a new business model, the development of a breakthrough product, the mega-merger, or a world-changing new technology. When it comes to growth, managers often think they have to "break the paradigm"; they say such things as, "If I can't get a double-digit gain by next year, it's not worth the effort." It's all or nothing. A single or double just doesn't seem good enough.

I have talked to literally hundreds of managers over the past few years who believe this, and they all are frustrated. They are strug-

---

* Whenever I use the terms "revenue" or "revenue growth," I mean profitable revenue or profitable revenue growth that uses capital efficiently.

gling to come up with the big ideas, and far too often, to extend the baseball metaphor, they swing and miss. Or worse, they don't even swing, failing to fund new ideas because of the perception that the risk is too great.

As I probed deeper into the problem, what I began to see is that managers in many companies do not have as effective a handle as they should on the building blocks for growth and the linkages between them.

In many cases these building blocks, such as development of new products and services, an effective sales force, finding ways to understand what the customer values, and segmenting markets, have been neglected and given inadequate resources. They are, in fact, not even on the radar screen of senior management to the same degree as cost reduction has been. Imagine what would happen if the same focus was given to sources of revenue growth as has been given to programs such as Six Sigma, centralized purchasing, and moving production facilities to low-cost countries to achieve global cost parity.

To get people to take a fresh look at the fundamentals and their importance for sustained revenue growth, I would, in one-on-one meetings, ask—on a scale of one to ten—questions like:

- What are you doing to help your customers prosper?
- What is the quality of your sales force in shaping and customizing a unique value proposition for your customer?
- How effectively is your pricing tied to the attributes the customer most highly values?
- In every interaction with a customer, how well do your people extract information about customer needs? Are they relaying the information to the people who can act on it, the departments that can develop products and services to satisfy those needs?

More often than not, when I ask these questions, the answer is on the lower end of the scale—a two, three, or four. Then the lightbulb comes on and what people begin to realize is that "we have met the enemy and they are us," that the answer to growth is not some silver bullet but lies within the business. *They come to understand that they are missing the obvious.* There's a deep sigh of relief when they come to realize that revenue growth is within their reach. In other words, what is missing is attention to the way the fundamentals of the business have to link to each other to make growth happen. Here we are going to supply that missing link. This is not a book about shifting your strategy or changing your business model, but how you can accelerate the revenue growth of your current business.

It often comes as a revelation to many of the people I work with that revenue growth is not just the domain of the specialists—the sales force or those in charge of product development, for example. Growth is everyone's business. Just as in baseball, where everyone on the team has the potential ability to hit a single or a double, in business, everyone—and that can run the gamut from the CEO to the marketing and sales people on the front end to those who have operations and service jobs on the back end—has an opportunity to increase revenues. And, in fact, people who don't occupy the executive suite have a big vested interest in doing so. Without growth, personal opportunity is a zero-sum game, that is, for me to win, someone else in the company (usually) has to lose. With growth, the organization expands and people can build a career and a future with a company they have faith in.

In the pages ahead, I am going to show you that you can follow a more effective growth process, one based on "singles and doubles" that will cumulatively over time enable you to increase your revenues substantially.

Singles and doubles are based on improvements or natural extensions of a business's strategy, business model, or technology. They can come from both relatively small day-to-day wins as well as adaptation to major changes in the marketplace. I am going to put this idea into context as well as provide tools that you can employ to increase your revenues and grow faster than the economy as a whole, no matter what business you are in. There are companies whose strategy is at a crossroads. Sun and Motorola are two examples. And there are industries, such as the music business, in which the current business model is obsolete. Even in these cases, singles and doubles provide the foundation for making the necessary change.

How you can make those changes is what this book is all about. Chapter 2 provides the reorientation from waiting for home runs to showing how to set realistic goals that you can achieve through singles and doubles and by making revenue growth everyone's business. Chapter 3 shows how to distinguish good growth—growth that is organic, profitable, differentiated, sustainable—from bad growth. Chapter 4 looks at how to dispel the myths and beliefs that inhibit organizations from growth.

Chapters 6 through 10 delve into specific tools of growth. Taken together and executed well day in and day out, they are a driver for accelerating revenue growth. Specifically, *revenue productivity* shows how to release creativity and grow revenues without increasing the amount of resources invested. The *growth budget* brings discipline to the management and creation of revenue growth and its linkage to budget commitments and tradeoffs between the short and long term. *Upstream marketing* pinpoints the specific needs of selected customer segments and how to satisfy them on a profitable basis better than the competition. *Cross-selling* shows how to present existing customers with a compelling reason to buy additional products and services (and then delivering that value proposition better than the competition). The *social engine* is the tool for synchronizing the people of the different silos of business (marketing, sales, product development, finance, etc.) so they are all on the same path for achieving revenue growth. *Converting innovation into revenue growth* builds on the ideas developed about the social engine to show how to select, nurture, and launch the ideas that will result in revenue growth over the short, medium, and long terms.

The time has come to provide a common approach that enables people inside the business to grow revenues on a routine basis. Cost-productivity approaches like Six Sigma are formal programs requiring certification. While I'm not proposing anything as rigid for revenue growth, what I believe will make a difference is a common language and program that will make growth everyone's business. That's exactly what you will find here in the pages ahead, distilled from my daily interactions with companies around the world.

Growth is the juice of human life. My hope is that this book serves two related purposes. One is to help businesses prosper, the other to help individuals personally grow. If companies achieve profitable, organic growth, it will have a buoyant effect, all other things being equal, on employment levels and the opportunity for individuals to build and expand their personal capacity.

Let me tell you what I've learned.

1

The Challenge of Profitable
Revenue Growth

G ROWTH IS the elusive goal at the top of everyone's agenda.
There are three reasons why it's proving difficult to achieve.

First, the balance has gone too far in the direction of cost-cutting
at the expense of revenue growth. More thought and time have been
given to tools like Six Sigma and actions like restructuring, achieving size through acquisition, and looking for opportunities to consol-
idate in an industry undergoing upheaval than to revenue growth.

Second, when most managers do think about growth, it is in terms
of home runs—the disruptive technology, the new revolutionary business model, the mega-merger—instead of the singles and doubles
that, when executed at a steady pace, cumulatively can increase revenues substantially.

Third, improving productivity and increasing revenues are seen as two separate issues, when they are, in fact, inseparable for long-term success. If managers concentrate only on raising productivity, they are doing only half their job.

Improving productivity means that a business finds a better way to do something that results in the enhancement of its competitive position and/or the creation of new opportunity, *while at the same time producing funding that can fuel its growth.* In contrast, sporadic, deep cost-cutting—downsizing, closing plants, across-the-board budget cuts—are one-shot reductions (often without attention to the consequences for revenue growth) that do not result in doing things in a better way. Cost-reduction campaigns are largely a result of the lack of discipline of productivity improvement on a long-term consistent basis. When employees experience these cost-reduction campaigns every year and sometimes two or three times a year and revenues are flat or declining, they know they are in a business going nowhere. It becomes a personal-survival issue and saps their emotional energy.

That's just how Bill Carter felt. He could already feel the acid churning in his stomach. The reason was simple: It was about to happen again.

Until nine months before, Carter, a store manager for the Furniture Globe chain, thought he had the best job in the world. As the person in charge of the "place to go for all your home furniture needs," he had for twelve years supervised what he thought of as "his store" in suburban Miami. He had turned in steadily increasing sales and earnings numbers year after year. He was always in the top 10 percent every time the 217-store retailer ranked the performance of each of its store managers.

But what Carter really loved was the joy he experienced in growing the business. Every time friends would ask why he had turned down opportunities for advancement from more important retail chains, he cited the thrill of being able to make his decisions in a growth business. For example, he was given the freedom and had substantial discretion to source merchandise that matched the needs of the unique demographics of his market, well-to-do Hispanics. This discretion drove his creative juices to ever-higher levels as he strove to grow revenues and be the largest and best retailer in the community. Not only were revenues increasing, but Carter was experiencing personal growth as well.

Carter couldn't see himself ever leaving Furniture Globe.

And then everything changed. Furniture Globe was acquired at an exorbitant price by a Fortune 100 conglomerate. For a few weeks, it seemed that nothing major was going to change—then the real overhaul began.

To help pay for the acquisition, the new parent company announced a mandatory, across-the-board, 8 percent head-count reduction. It meant that Carter had to reduce his staff by ten people. He knew this would not only affect his sales growth—there would be fewer employees to take care of customers—but that it was the first shot in destroying the *esprit de corps* of his store.

Then the other shoe dropped. Corporate announced that all decisions about buying merchandise, advertising, and the mix and quantity of stock units and when they would be delivered to individual stores would be centralized. Carter sensed that the company was now focused on cost reductions and cash generation instead of searching for profitable revenue growth. In his gut, he knew that his sales growth engine would start running out of gas.

He was right. Not too long thereafter, both sales growth and buzz about the store began to decline. More customers walked out without buying anything. The number of people coming in to the store also went downhill. Customers began to complain that the store's selection had been cut and skewed the wrong way, not meeting the tastes of the store's Hispanic customer base.

The problem really hit home when he saw the couple who were right out of central casting. They were in their early forties, and even though they were in casual clothes—she in designer jeans, he in a wrinkled nylon running suit—he could tell they were well-off.

The couple was looking seriously at the highest-end outdoor furniture the store sold. They were searching around for sales help, when Carter spotted them. They weren't having any luck, and Carter knew why.

The decision to cut staff was coming home to roost as he saw the couple walk out of the store.

Does this experience sound familiar even if you have never been through an acquisition or merger? Bill Carter's experience at Furniture Globe shows both the business and personal consequences of being part of a business that is growing or one that is not. It also shows that we need to think differently when it comes to finding ways to grow.

Profitable, sustained revenue growth results from a mind-set that differs significantly from one required for either cost-cutting or productivity improvement. The latter are deterministic and internally driven, while growth requires creativity and the ability to look at a business from the outside in.

Growth is a creative act, but it is also a social process that is disciplined and links together the moving parts of an organization to achieve a consistent increase in revenues. It has at its core ten tools that you can start using this Monday morning. Here's an overview.

THE TEN TOOLS OF
PROFITABLE REVENUE GROWTH

1. **Revenue growth is everyone's business, so make it part of everyone's daily work routine.** Every employee wants to be part of a company's growth agenda, but most don't know how. Managers need to provide them with both information and tools, starting with making revenue growth an inherent part of daily conversations, meetings, and presentations.

   Just as everyone participates in cost reduction, so must everyone be engaged in the growth agenda of the business. Every contact of every employee with a customer is an opportunity for revenue growth: The people answering the phones in the call-center can provide valuable information on unmet customer needs. The appliance repair person can discover patterns and timing of demand for replacement of appliances. Salespeople can extract market intelligence and ensure that it is communicated to the product development, operations, and service departments. Logistics people, through on-time deliveries, can help stores avoid stock-outs, thus enhancing customer satisfaction, an important foundation of future revenue growth.

   The fruits of these efforts for revenue growth energize people and enhance their self-confidence. Growth taps into all their latent energy to generate ideas that can carry the organization to higher levels of growth. Growth truly is everyone's business, not something that is solely the concern of management. Every employee at every level can be doing something for a customer.

2. **Hit many singles and doubles, not just home runs.** While home runs provide the opportunity for a quantum increase in the

growth trajectory, they are unpredictable and don't happen all the time. Singles and doubles, however, can happen every day of the year. They result from a determined, day-in and day-out improvement in the activities and social processes of a company; they form the drivers of profitable revenue growth.

Increasing revenues through singles and doubles build a growth mind-set throughout the business, so that when the opportunity for a home run does come along, you'll be better prepared to take advantage of it.

For example, Dell's efforts, beginning in 1993, to improve inventory turns to use less cash and reduce price and product obsolescence began as a single. The company's initial goal was to increase inventory turns, which were averaging six a year, to ten. Over the last ten years, Dell has continuously improved the totality of its supply chain so that its inventory turns over one hundred times a year, or once less than every four days. The result is higher revenue growth and what has become a lethal competitive weapon against all PC manufacturers. In addition, this supply chain enables Dell to accelerate revenue growth by entering into new market opportunities like printers, servers, and storage.

3. **Seek good growth and avoid bad growth.** A framework for distinguishing good from bad growth is a crucial element in generating revenue growth. Good growth not only increases revenues but improves profits, is sustainable over time, and does not use unacceptable levels of capital. It is also primarily organic (internally generated) and based on differentiated products and services that fill new or unmet needs, creating value for customers.

The ability to generate internal growth separates leaders who build their businesses on a solid foundation of long-term profitable growth from those who, through acquisitions and financial engineering, increase revenues like crazy but who create that growth on shaky footings that ultimately crumble. Many acquisitions provide a one-shot improvement, as duplicative costs are removed from the combined companies. But few, if any, demonstrate any significant improvement in the *rate* of growth of revenues.

4. **Dispel the myths that inhibit both people and organizations from growing.** An important part of any leader's role is to realistically confront excuses such as: "We are in a no-growth industry, and no one is growing"; "Customers are buying only on price"; or "The distributors are the ones in direct contact with retailers, and there's not much I can do." Every leader needs a growth agenda and the ability to communicate an urgency about the need to increase revenues and build the business so that action-oriented people within the organization find out what needs to be done *today*.

5. **Turn the idea of productivity on its head by increasing revenue productivity.** The old saw says "we have to do more with less." The problem, though, is that the focus is usually on the "less" and the "more" rarely happens. Revenue productivity is a tool for getting that elusive "more" by actively and creatively searching for ideas for revenue growth without using a disproportionate amount of resources. It shows how to invest your current level of resources in a way that leads to increased sales by analyzing everything a business does, from the seemingly mundane to the vitally important.

6. **Develop and implement a growth budget.** All companies have a budget. It is, however, astonishing how little detail about revenue and sources of revenue growth you can find there. Almost all of the lines in the budget are cost-related. Few, if any, identify resources explicitly earmarked for growth. The growth budget provides a foundation that will allow a company to increase revenues instead of just talking about it. It includes all critical actions over the short, medium, and long terms that require resources to achieve revenue growth goals. And there is follow-through that includes rewards for success and penalties for poor performance.

7. **Beef up upstream marketing.** One of the key missing links for generating revenue growth at most companies is upstream marketing. What most people visualize as marketing involves advertising, promotion, brand-building, and communicating with customers through public relations, trade shows, and in-store displays. Those activities are obviously of great importance but primarily "downstream" in nature—that is, they enhance the acceptance of a product or service that already exists. Upstream marketing, on the other hand, takes place at a much earlier stage by developing a clear market segmentation map and then identifying and precisely defining which customer segments to focus on. It analyzes how the end-user uses the product or service and what competitive advantage will be required to win the customer and at what price points.

8. **Understand how to do effective cross-selling (or value/ solutions selling).** Cross-selling can be a significant source of revenue growth, but most companies approach it from exactly the *wrong* perspective. They start by saying, "What else can we

sell to our existing customer base?" However, instead of looking inside-out your organization, you need to look outside-in. Successful cross-selling starts by selecting a segment of customers and then working backward to define precisely the mix of products and services they need and creatively shaping a value proposition unique to them. Effective cross-selling ensures the proposition is presented to the right decision makers in the language of the customer and spells out the financial, physical, and post-purchase benefits of the offering.

9. **Create a social engine to accelerate revenue growth.** Every organization is a social system, the center of which is a way of thinking and acting that sets both day-to-day actions and the long-term agenda. When an organization has an explicit growth agenda understood by everyone, growth becomes a central focus—a social engine—during formal meetings as well as informal discussions. The social engine is then fueled by growth ideas as one growth initiative builds on another. People at all levels then see growth as everyone's job. The social engine and its associated tools provide the mechanism for making revenue growth a reality by developing a laser-sharp focus, aligning individual silo priorities and *making the right tradeoffs*.

10. **Operationalize innovation by converting ideas into revenue growth.** Innovation is not the private property of lone geniuses working apart from the mainstream of the business. In any company of reasonable size, innovation is a social process that requires collaboration and communication for idea generation, selecting those ideas for revenue growth that are to be funded, and shaping those ideas into product prototypes and launching them into the marketplace.

The tools that have been outlined are the foundation of your program for future revenue growth. But remember what we said earlier. Revenue growth and productivity improvement are not conflicting goals. To keep the revenue growth engine running, you must have a disciplined day-in and day-out program of cost productivity improvement. Not only is it imperative for competitive advantage, it provides the findings for future growth.

The following chapter presents one of the core ideas of this book, the imperative of creating singles and doubles as the primary basis of your future revenue growth. We'll use several examples, beginning with a major player in its industry who, by only swinging for the fences, was frustrated over a three-year period as it failed to meet its revenue growth goals. When it started hitting a lot of singles and doubles, a gush of energy flowed through the organization and sales soared.

2

Reorient Your Thinking About Growth: Hit Many Singles and Doubles, Not Just Home Runs

ARE YOU oriented the right way when it comes to finding growth opportunities on a day-in and day-out basis? At most companies, people are not. The first thing to change is your mind-set. Instead of thinking about growth in terms of finding the mega-idea, you need to see the value in "singles and doubles," small growth projects and ideas that can have a huge impact cumulatively. Second, you need to realize that there is "good growth" and "bad growth." And, finally, you need to confront the enemy within your organization, the people and mind-set that say "growth is not possible for us."

Let's meet a company that changed its mind-set when it came to finding growth, making increasing revenues part of the corporate DNA every day.

Avery Dennison is one of many companies that have created bottom-line growth through aggressive cost productivity and acquisitions. However, as the twenty-first century approached, chairman and CEO Philip M. Neal began to see the imperative of revenue growth and making growth everyone's job. The journey to profitable revenue growth, however, was filled with many false starts.

Some background is in order. Profits at the Pasadena, California–based company—with $4.2 billion in annual sales, the global leader in pressure-sensitive technology and self-adhesives used in labeling materials and consumer products—had steadily increased throughout the 1990s as a direct result of cutting costs ahead of the competition. Excellent bottom-line growth resulted, and the company's stock price increased accordingly.

But Phil Neal realized that cost productivity improvements alone would not be enough to maintain or improve the share price of Avery Dennison's stock. Without consistent top-line growth, a business eventually runs out of opportunities to become substantially more efficient. Just as bad, the best people in the organization start to leave because they understand that a company that is not growing offers fewer career opportunities.

Looking to move quickly to prevent all those problems, Neal began to push each of his five division managers for top-line growth. He asked for—and received—commitments based on mutually agreed-upon growth targets.

His focus was on home runs, the big breakthrough new products that would contribute *a minimum* of $50 million to the top line relatively quickly. At a $4.2 billion company, searching for projects of at least that size seemed reasonable. In fact, the thinking was that if you didn't aim for growth projects that big, it wasn't worth the time or effort.

In setting these extremely ambitious goals, the practice at Avery

Dennison—as it is at most companies—was to take the revenue results of the just-completed year, tack on some percentage, and announce the new sales objective. ("Let's see, you did $500 million last year. We want 10 percent growth, so that makes it $550 million for the year ahead.") The specific ideas that could produce growth, how growth would be funded, who would be in charge of the growth initiatives, and how progress along the way would be assessed were left to the individual business unit managers to figure out on their own.

Again, Avery Dennison was like most companies in this regard, and up until this point it hadn't mattered. None of that precision had been required in the past. Neal, working with senior management, had always set growth targets, and his managers would then deliver bull's-eyes, or close to them.

However, over the last three years it wasn't happening, even though the enthusiasm for growth was solid. Avery Dennison had a typical three-year strategic plan that promised double-digit growth based on unspecified breakthrough projects. However, while the business-unit managers were meeting bottom-line objectives, they were falling short of what was needed for top-line revenue growth. Those unspecified $50 million (minimum) breakthroughs weren't happening.

Neal increased the jawboning. Nothing. He asked for and received more reports on the status of the growth projects. He made it a point to talk about growth as he visited every part of the organization. And nothing changed, except his level of frustration, which continued to rise.

What was even worse, Neal, a Stanford MBA, and a former McKinsey consultant, couldn't understand why growth wasn't happening. There was no one factor holding back the sales of his company's products. Sure, a sluggish economy had something to do with it; so did increasing competition. But Avery Dennison had dealt successfully with cyclical economies and competition before.

Phil Neal brought in top consultants who tried to coach his people in thinking out of the box to create new business models and to teach them about new disruptive technologies that would result in breakthrough products. Still, nothing happened. And the CEO grew more and more frustrated until he finally figured out what the two problems were.

First, Neal came to realize that he had not put into place a system or processes his managers and employees could follow to ensure that revenue growth would happen.

"I had never given them a process, a framework they could use as we tried to grow," Neal says. "So I shouldn't have been surprised that they didn't know exactly what they needed to do."

The second problem was the focus Neal and his executive team had placed on hitting home runs, the big breakthroughs aimed at bringing that additional $50 million (minimum) into the corporation. As Neal puts it, "We spun a lot of wheels, wasted a lot of money, and lost time in our attempt to try to hit them out of the park."

Faced with clear evidence that the traditional approach wasn't working, Neal turned Avery Dennison around 180 degrees. He decided things needed to be done differently. His first move? Putting processes in place that would create singles and doubles, realizing that was the best way to gain traction when it came to producing growth on a consistent basis.

SINGLES AND DOUBLES

In baseball, the home run, especially in crucial, big-game situations, is electrifying and exciting. In business, the big bold idea, the breakthrough disruptive technology, the new product that will revolutionize the marketplace, the new business model that will change the game, the next new thing, are similarly exhilarating. But there is a problem: *Home runs don't happen every day or even every decade.* And they frequently come in cycles. At a company like DuPont, developing breakthroughs such as Kevlar or Teflon may be a once-a-decade phenomenon. Even as disciplined, rigorous, and consistent as the drug discovery and development processes are in pharmaceuticals, the blockbusters don't happen every day or even every year. Despite their size and scale, the big pharmaceutical companies go through cycles of feast and famine.

A surer and more consistent path—one that does not exclude home runs—is what I call going for "singles and doubles," growth based on improvements or natural extensions of the strategy, business model, customer needs, or technology of a business. These singles and doubles can come from adapting to major changes in the marketplace as well as relatively small day-to-day wins. The latter will be illustrated by the "hundred day" program at Avery Dennison, which will be discussed below, the former by examples that follow later in this chapter, such as Cardinal Health's repositioning of its surgical-glove business.

Singles and doubles come from disciplined, creative, and innovative in-depth analyses of *all* the fundamentals of a business, including new ways of identifying undermet or unmet customer needs and meeting them through improved internal alignment of the company. (This is something we will explain in detail in Chapter 9.)

Singles and doubles *do not* come from a look in the rearview mirror, extrapolating from what has been done in the past. Rather, they are a result of looking at the business from the outside-in, from customer needs backward into the company. The impact of singles and doubles can be huge. In fact, they form the *foundation* for the home run—they provide a business with the discipline of execution, which is absolutely necessary to successfully bring a breakthrough technology to market or to implement a new business model.

AVERY DENNISON

Phil Neal embraced the concept of singles and doubles and put a process in place to translate the idea into action. He created a series of pilot teams in various divisions throughout the company, each team composed of people from all departments within that division. He charged each team with getting a small revenue growth project up and running within one hundred days. Size did not matter. Some of the projects would generate only $250,000 in additional revenues at first. But what was mandatory was that each team had a sales order, a commitment from a customer to buy, in hand in a little over three months.

The one-hundred-day deadline is vital, because it forces everyone to immediately confront issues that can keep the team from succeeding. It also forces employees to break down the walls that separate departments. Indeed, as Tom Van Dessel, one of Avery Dennison's managers for strategic growth, points out, one of the first things one of the company's divisions does, when faced with the necessity of creating a growth project quickly, is to create a team from all the possible departments affected—technology, service, operations, marketing, and so on. And whenever possible, Avery Dennison tries to include a potential customer on the team so that the company can be sure it is focused on the market's needs.

"We say to the team leader: Here are your resources—the people we have assigned—and you have your deadline. Now, go do it," Van Dessel explains. "*How* they do it is up to the team."

When you have less than four months to come up with a new

growth project, you can't wait two weeks for someone in marketing to get back to you on the preliminary results of, say, a focus group. And you don't fool around making sure the prototype is perfect. You do the best you can in the time available—and if that is 70 percent of the finished product, it is 70 percent—and you take what you have, a very rough prototype, and test it with customers to see what they like and what they don't and make the modifications accordingly. There is huge psychological power in imposing a real deadline.

At the Ohio plant, a salesman was put in charge of the one-hundred-day project. This often makes sense. Good salespeople know not only what is going on with their customers—something we talk about later in the chapter—but also who within their own companies can help satisfy their customers' needs.

It certainly worked in Ohio. The project was designed to solve a problem for Procter & Gamble, which wanted to attach a sample of a new product to one of its best-sellers. P&G's thinking was that if you liked the first product, you'd love the second, once you tried it. The problem? Existing adhesives strong enough to keep the sample in place during shipping were almost impossible to remove without damaging either the product or the sample once the consumer got the product home. The existing alternative, running a big strip of tape around the outside of both the product and sample, was unattractive from a merchandising point of view.

Within the self-imposed one-hundred-day deadline, the Avery Dennison Ohio plant developed a glue that both held the sample in place and was easy to remove. Not only did this generate revenues of $250,000, it gave Avery Dennison a new product that it could sell worldwide.

Success stories like the Ohio pilot project not only broke down the barriers between the departments at Avery Dennison, they also showed the rest of the company that it was possible to gain growth almost immediately. The wins were celebrated and held up as company-wide examples, which, not surprisingly, got a huge number of Avery Dennison employees volunteering to be in on the next growth project.

"That's a key point about this," Neal explains. "When some people hear that a project generates only $250,000 in sales, they are tempted to say, 'Why bother,' and there are a lot of answers to that. First, it is another $250,000 in revenues that we are adding at a time when the competition's sales are flat. Second, that project gets folded into our base. It is not a one-time thing, but an extra $250,000 every year. Third, invariably these projects work elsewhere. In the case of the adhesive, there might be twenty other customers we could sell it to, so now we are talking about not $250,000 annually but another $5 million a year. And finally, we are not doing one growth project at a time but many, with each of them also having the same opportunity to scale up."

In other words, all these gains build upon themselves. Neal now easily foresees a time when simple new growth projects will increase Avery Dennison's sales by 1 to 2 percent annually, a significant addition when added to its previous single-digit rate of revenue growth.

The nice thing about this approach, from the perspective of a manager such as Van Dessel, is the growth projects are not additional work. They replace a less productive part of their job. "When you take on a growth project, it forces you to reprioritize what needs to be done," he says. "The growth project goes to the top of the list and pushes everything down a rung. What is at the bottom, something that was not adding much value, falls away."

The Avery Dennison story is significant on several levels. First, a potential $5 million increase on the base of the Ohio plant's current revenues is very significant. Second, the singles and doubles process brought a focus on the part of the people on the pilot teams to what customers were saying about their needs It helped them to realign their priorities, forcing them to make tradeoffs to meet those needs. It makes a reality of what has been called the horizontal or customer-centric organization. Third, while the pilot projects focused on short-term revenue growth, Neal also put in place separate processes for medium (one to three) years and long (three to five years) revenue growth.

Phil Neal's frustration began to subside as he sensed the high energy in the company that resulted from the growth projects. His reviews of each of his businesses have changed to focus on profitable revenue growth. The metrics for how the business is measured, the criteria for who gets promoted and how incentives are awarded, have also changed to ensure that the commitment to growth becomes part of Avery Dennison's DNA.

HOW EVERY PART OF THE BUSINESS CAN CREATE SINGLES AND DOUBLES FOR REVENUE GROWTH

Leadership creates the environment for all parts of the organization to connect and participate in a growth program based on singles and doubles. The legendary Sam Walton had regular Saturday meetings that included not only the top managers of Wal-Mart but also store managers, the managers of functional areas like finance and logistics and vendors. The focus of these four-hour sessions was to create the emotional and intellectual energy for singles and doubles that would help Wal-Mart outgrow the competition. Leaders like Walton want everyone to think about growth, to propose ideas for growth, and to participate in growth projects.

One of the major ways in which any part of a business can contribute to revenue growth through singles and doubles is by making effective linkages with other critical parts of the organization. For example, linking the unfiltered intelligence gathered by the sales force to people in upstream marketing (the people who figure out what customer segments to target) and product development enables you to better detect shifts in customer usage and buying behavior that can result in new ideas for growth. Linking people in customer service, especially those who deal with customer complaints, to those in operations to provide information on defective products is imperative for correcting problems that drive away customers and decrease revenues.

Better customer service results in both cost-productivity and market-share increases, which leads to revenue growth. And, of course, people in customer service can identify the sorts of products and services customers are asking for that you don't currently have. A happy customer is usually a repeat customer.

But even an unhappy customer can be a source of singles and doubles, of profitable revenue growth, if the linkages between the appropriate departments are in place. That is exactly what happened at NETg, a division of the Thomson Corporation.

Like most on-line e-learning companies, NETg saw a rapid defection of customers in the late 1990s and into this century, as the reality of the on-line e-learning industry as a whole failed to live up to the hype.

"When I came in as president, I launched a back-to-basics movement," says Joe Dougherty, "and looked at the business from a new angle."

It was readily apparent to Dougherty that costs had to be cut. But without revenue growth, the business would go into a nosedive. In seeking out new sources of revenue growth, he set out to understand why customers left NETg. A primary reason was that clients—many of them Fortune 1,000 companies—spent a lot of money putting e-learning opportunities in place, but their employees weren't using them.

The question, of course, was why. Dougherty invested a significant amount of money in a study by an outside consulting firm to find the answer.

The problem wasn't the content, but the process. The study revealed that customers frequently could not access NETg's learning system. There were often conflicts between NETg's software, that provide the course material, and the company computers on which it had to run. The end result was that customers could not get to the course content material. If they couldn't access it, they couldn't use it. And if they weren't using it, companies saw no reason to continue paying for it.

"It was a blinding glimpse of the obvious," is the way Dougherty put it. "Our people always described us as a content provider, but the content doesn't do people any good if they can't get to it."

Instead of just reacting to customer complaints when the software didn't work, Dougherty invested the resources to develop systems that would link seamlessly with those of his customers and he reoriented the priorities of departments within the company to focus on providing customers with that seamless access.

"It turns out that we had the skill—the ability to integrate with a customer's system—but we weren't taking advantage of it," Dougherty says. NETg is now giving customers a reason to continue doing business with the firm. It is an almost mundane, but highly illustrative example of a single and double. So is the way Staples is using its existing assets a little more effectively.

Just about every Staples store has a photocopy and printing center. The problem, as the $12 billion office supply chain discovered, is that a significant number of its customers didn't think of Staples when it came to getting printing or photocopying done. "Awareness was extremely low," says John J. Mahoney, Staples executive vice president and chief administrative officer. And those customers (who had never used the service) wondered about the quality.

"Let me give you a personal anecdote," Mahoney says. "My wife was with a friend of hers and her friend's daughter. The daughter had just finished an important college paper that she needed to present to her class. She needed photocopies, so she went to the local copy center in town, which told her it could not get it done in time. My wife said, 'Why don't you take it to the nearby Staples store,' and her friend said, 'Oh no, this is important, we want quality.' She had the impression that our copying department was like going to the drugstore and putting the coin in the machine. Well, they ended up going to Staples, and she could not have been happier with the results."

Getting that message out—that Staples does the highest quality work and does it quickly and affordably—is something that the chain has been working on and it's paying off. Initial results show that greater awareness and usage of the copying/printing centers are increasing a store's total sales by 1 percent to 3 percent a year. If we use 2 percent as an average, that means a yearly gain of $240 million in revenues.

As the Staples and NETg examples show, each part of the business should be engaged in creating singles and doubles for revenue growth. This includes not only the "usual suspects" of the sales force, marketing, and product development, but also areas in which you might least expect to be sources of revenue growth. These include finance, billing, legal, operations (manufacturing), customer service, and logistics. What follows is by no means an exhaustive list of areas and functions that can contribute. In fact, it just scratches the surface and is meant to be the stimulus for how you can create singles and doubles in your own business. To help stimulate that discussion, I have included a series of questions for each area or function.

1. **The sales force.** Is your sales force focused on finding out what your company can do for its customers? Are your salespeople focused on the customers with the best potential? Does the sales force have too many products? Are territories too big or small? If organized on a geographic basis, should the sales force be reconfigured by customer industry?

2. **Helping your customers grow.** Does the sales force understand your customer's decision-making processes and social networks? Are you examining the problems and opportunities of your customers and applying your intellectual capital to help them grow their business? Is your organization internally connected (e.g., product development people know what marketing people are observing about customers) so that you are able to share strategic launch information with customers and work together to develop joint marketing plans and enhance the revenues of both companies? If the customer is large enough, do you have a salesperson in residence who knows everything happening at the customer's shop to understand its pressures and the opportunities these pressures present you? That way, when the customer grows, you grow. Jeff Immelt, the CEO of General Electric, has expressed this as "ACFC"—at the customer, for the

customer— an idea he is implanting in all the businesses of the company. (We will explore this concept in detail later.)

3. **Customer-need segmentation.** Do you have the right skills in customer-need segmentation to refresh, extend, and reposition your products? Are you using segmentation skills to do further subsegmentation to discover new customers for your current products? (Because this subject is so important, we will return to it later.)

4. **Pricing.** Does your pricing structure reflect the value you provide customers? Does it also simultaneously improve revenue growth and the bottom line through effectively segmenting the customer's buying behavior and identifying the attributes the customer most values?

5. **Positioning and, where necessary, repositioning your business.** Does your position in the marketplace make you vulnerable to new competitors such as the way Dell has encroached on Sun Microsystems in the server market; to new technologies such as wireless in the local telephone wirelines market; and macroeconomic factors such as currency exchange rate imbalances?

6. **Downstream marketing.** How well are you using branding, advertising, and promotion to enhance revenues and change perceptions of your products? Does your advertising change the consumer's view of your brand from what it is to what it should be?

7. **Customer satisfaction.** Are you providing pre-purchase (e.g., delivery on time, the full order, proper billing) and post-purchase customer service better than the competition? This can be a cause and effect of revenue growth. Customer satisfaction is an emotional experience etched in the consumer's mind. He may not remember the details, but satisfied customers are more

likely to be repeat buyers and also create word-of-mouth. There is no better generator of revenues than a customer emotionally articulating the experience to someone else. What kind of experience are you providing to your customers?

8. **Logistics and delivery operations.** One hundred percent reliability increases the chances for suppliers to get preference over the competition for additional shelf space from retailers. This is a critical foundation for revenue growth. How reliable is your organization? How *exactly* do you know?

9. **Manufacturing.** Are your production processes and tools like lean manufacturing giving you an edge? A persistent, faster drive to achieve global cost advantage ahead of competitors gains market share without negatively affecting the bottom line. Similarly, achieving a differentiation in delivery to the customer and at the same time substantially better inventory turns than the competition gains market share and revenue growth without price wars. How good are you in both areas? No matter how you answer, what are you doing to improve?

10. **Finance.** People in finance have special skills that can be valuable in helping the sales force shape value propositions in the language of business—cash flow, return on investment, margin, asset turns, and the linkages between them. Are you using them to the fullest?

11. **Billing.** One of the greatest issues for any business is untimely, inaccurate, and incomplete billing, a source of frustration for both the sales force and customers. Often, disputes are resolved through reduction in revenues leading to reduction in margins and the bottom line. Making sure this doesn't happen is certainly low-hanging fruit that can help increase revenues. When was the last time you took a look at how your company

handled billing (other than to resolve a problem)? Billing should be reviewed on a consistent and on-going basis.

12. **Legal.** Lawyers often have good business acumen and are the source of ideas for structuring contracts so they increase revenue growth. Contacts with their counterparts in a customer's organization can often provide information useful in detecting the customer's decision-making processes. Is your legal department doing any of this? If not, why not?

13. **Information technology.** Information technology is at the heart of growth for companies such as Amazon.com, eBay, American Express, and Wal-Mart. Is *your* information technology department providing you with real-time updates about what customers are buying? Is it analyzing what the competition is doing? Is it spotting opportunities for cross-selling? A growth agenda provides the opportunity for people in IT to become fully integrated in every part of the organization's operation.

14. **Human resources.** Of course, HR needs to be involved with the issues associated with pensions, benefits, health care costs, and leadership development. But there are a few HR departments such as Bank of America's, in an effort spearheaded by Jim Shanley, that are fostering the social linkages that break down the walls between the different silos of the organization. Is your HR team making sure, for example, that the information the sales force learns from customers is being fed directly to product development and marketing?

As described above, obtaining singles and doubles requires everyone engaging and committing to make them happen. Managers at all levels need to examine every activity they—and their people—carry out, and ask what needs to be changed to increase profitable revenue growth. These changes build momentum. Employees can see your sales steadily increase, and, as we have said, you also lay the foundation for potential home runs.

The more singles and doubles you actually hit, the greater the opportunity will be that their cumulative effect will increase the distance between you and your next competitor. It also changes the psyche and energy of your organization.

HOW A SINGLE AND DOUBLE CAN BECOME A HOME RUN

Companies that are customer-centric and have a growth culture convert adverse market situations into new opportunities for singles and doubles through (among other things) re-segmenting and repositioning. Cardinal Health, for example, had to rethink its medical-glove business. Sales at the $200 million division of the $4 billion company had been essentially flat for ten years. The problem was that its traditional glove (what your dentist puts on his hands before he says "open wide") was rapidly losing its differentiation and was becoming a commodity, primarily due to extreme pricing pressure from Chinese imports. In this highly capital-intensive business, Cardinal found that its margins were being dramatically reduced and that its return on investment was therefore unacceptable. The traditional options were clear. Cardinal could let the low end simply slip away, taking out as much cash as it could until the business went dry. Or it could stick with the low-end glove business, cutting enough cost (continuously) to eke out a profit.

Ron Labrum of Cardinal's Medical-Surgical Products and Services segment, which includes gloves, describes the simple alternative the company chose: "To stay in the market, we made the decision to buy versus continuing to make those 'basic' kinds of gloves. It was a very troublesome decision, but fear of being driven out of business forced us to make it."

As Michael A. Lynch, president of the gloves division, puts it: "If you are not a leader, you're a loser, and it was clear that we were never going to be a leader if we made the gloves ourselves. As painful as it was, we decided to outsource the manufacturing of them."

Lynch went on the attack and decided to reposition the total glove business. He focused his energies on the higher margin surgical-glove segment of the business, investing the necessary management time and skills, financial resources, and technology. The money for that move came from the capital freed up by outsourcing the low-end gloves. His division increased its total glove market-share revenues and profits. The total glove division sales climbed nearly 4 percent in 2002 and another 10 percent in 2003 at a time when overall industry sales were up just 2 percent. Its market share increased accordingly. The move increased profits two ways. Not only was Cardinal able to sell more of the higher-margin, higher-priced surgical gloves—its costs fell because of productivity improvements.

In converting this adversity into opportunity, Cardinal's single and double of figuring out a simple way of saving its low-end glove business provided the platform for what became a home run. It freed up managerial attention and capital for investment elsewhere. Success in this segment against the Chinese threat got Lynch and his team to reposition Cardinal to attack the higher margin, higher revenue surgical glove market and succeed. The result? A stronger, broader, and more profitable hold on the market that is clearly a home run.

Cardinal Health shows how a company can convert a problem into an opportunity for revenue growth. Everyone can contribute to gaining greater revenues, as the following examples show.

HOW EVERYONE CAN GENERATE
IDEAS FOR REVENUE GROWTH

The growth box is a simple tool everyone should use for generating ideas for singles and doubles. It helps you avoid the trap of thinking only in terms of products, focusing instead on customer needs. Even better, it is extremely easy to use. It really can be done on the back of a napkin, over lunch, or when you have drinks with customers, people from other parts of the organization, suppliers such as your advertising agency, even noncompeting providers of products and services to your customers. Looking at the four quadrants of the growth box can trigger ideas for growing revenues and increasing profits. Let's use some examples to show how.

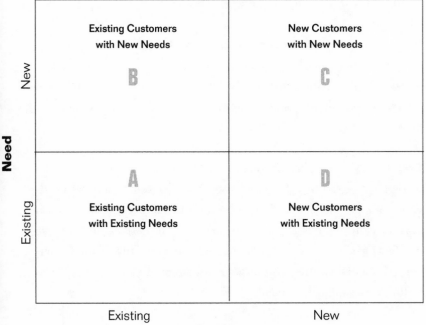

Box A (Existing Customers with Existing Needs)

Wal-Mart's move to serve exisiting customers with more than general merchandise by adding groceries to its offerings accelerated its revenue growth and made it the world's largest corporation. It's doing something similar by adding products found in Staples, Office Depot, and Home Depot. All these moves are designed to fill the needs of current customers.

Box D (New Customers with Existing Needs)

Avon is a great example of this method of increasing revenues. It identified teenage segments in the United States as a new customer segment it had not previously served and then used existing capabilities to serve them. It was an intiative that significantly improved Avon's level of revenues in the United States.

Box C (New Customers with New Needs)

When a company has to change its business model or strategy, it usually develops ideas for Box C; for example, an industrial-based business-to-business company moving into consumer products for the first time.

Box B (Existing Customers with New Needs)

Using its existing customer base, Avon looked at the personal-care products that it could potentially sell it to its customers but it currently did not carry. Avon then created the products to fill these needs. One simple example: Women have become increasingly concerned about cellulite, so the company created Cellu-Sculpt Anti-Cellulite Slimming Treatment.

EXPAND THE POND

An additional example of applying Box B (existing customers with new needs) is "expanding the pond"—visualizing a larger definition of customer need, of which you currently supply only a portion. This is especially appropriate when you have a dominant share of a narrowly defined market. You look to expand what you offer your customer base by expanding into related market segments. That literally means expanding the pond in which you fish for business, by redefining what you do for a living to be more inclusive while still remaining true to your core business. It is an additional source of creative ideas, because it explores the customer's need in a larger scope. For example, the continuing battle between Coke and Pepsi involves not just carbonated beverages, which constitute only 3 percent of the total fluids consumed per day. The battlefield now focuses on the other 97 percent, nonalcoholic beverages such as bottled water, juice, and athletic drinks. One question that could spur your thinking is: How can you redefine the scope of your market such that your 90 percent share in the old definition becomes 10 percent in the new definition?

Singles and doubles enable you to reorient the thinking of everyone in the business to achieve revenue growth day-in and day-out. Johnson Controls, as we are about to see, did just that.

HOW JOHNSON CONTROLS CHANGED
ITS SALES APPROACH TO INCREASE
REVENUE GROWTH

Through recruiting top executives who were team players, upgrading its sales force, and clearly segmenting customers, Brian J. Stark and his leadership team at Johnson Controls have recently increased the rate of growth of revenues and profits in its Controls Group, a leader in supplying and servicing buildings with heating, ventilating, air-conditioning (HVAC), lighting, security, and fire management systems. The group provides integrated facility management for many Fortune 500 companies. It manages more than one billion square feet worldwide and saves hundreds of millions of dollars in energy and operating costs for its customers. But that was not always the case.

The Controls Group had been selling energy-related hardware—a heating system here, air-conditioning there—based on price. When Stark became its president four years ago, he and his team saw a major opportunity in meeting the energy and facility operations requirements of big organizations like General Motors. Typically, these companies have many buildings and are extremely concerned about improving the productivity of their energy use. They also want to free up managerial attention from noncore activities like building maintenance, as well as make more capital available for use elsewhere.

But to act on the opportunity to sell energy systems, and to obtain long-term servicing contracts, required new sales capabilities. To be effective, the Johnson Controls sales team would have to analyze a building's total energy requirements and determine which application of technology or process change would improve energy productivity. The team would also need to analyze the behavioral patterns of people using the building and how this affects the use of energy.

The next step would be to develop a program for providing service on a 24/7 basis and a value proposition for the customer. This would require people on the team to have the financial skills to see the total picture and analyze how much cash flow and cost the customer would save with a long-term contract. In many cases, the team has to work with, negotiate, and eventually sell directly to the CFO of the company buying the energy solution from Johnson Controls. That's a far cry from just knocking 10 percent off of the contract price in order to sell a new project.

In addition, the chance to sell turn-key energy systems requires the sales team to be able to communicate effectively with Johnson's service and technical people.

The action steps Johnson Controls took to build the foundation for revenue growth included the following:

• Stark and HR vice president Darrell Middleton hired executives committed not only to the top and bottom lines but also to the team concept. Executive compensation was put on a team basis and people with big personal egos never made the cut. Stark and Middleton called this "eliminating the 'I' factor."

• A commitment to spending the resources to support and train the sales staff in solutions selling, especially showing them how to draw on various parts of the business in developing value propositions and building solutions for customers. These resources for training are part of the Johnson Controls growth budget (see Chapter 6 for more information about the growth budget).

• Intellectual honesty about which sales managers and sales-people would be able to operate successfully in this new environment of solutions selling. Stark and his team came to realize that no amount of training would bring some people to the required level of expertise. These people were either reassigned or let go.

• Recognize that salespeople who would have the capabilities to do solutions selling would command a higher level of compensation and possibly be recruited from nontraditional backgrounds.

• Building reference accounts to show new customers that proposed solutions from Johnson Controls would provide bottom-line impact and that local offices would deliver what was promised.

Through these key steps, Johnson Controls is now clearly differentiated from competitors, especially a major rival, which, until recently, has been cutting back its sales force. But the key differentiator is that the competition is primarily selling individual products, whereas Johnson Controls is selling solutions.

This chapter has focused on the importance of singles and doubles in making growth everyone's business. An equally important lesson is the quality of growth, the subject of our next chapter.

3

How to Tell Good Growth
from Bad Growth

ALL TOP-LINE GROWTH is *not* created equal. History has shown that most mergers and acquisitions do little to help the long-term health and revenue growth rate of an organization. Similarly, growth that uses capital inefficiently is not the way to go. The question is how can you tell good growth from bad? We will try to find an answer by looking at the example of Colgate-Palmolive.

For the past several years, Colgate-Palmolive has faced an exceptionally strong set of challenges—slow market growth, juggernaut competitors with huge resources, and ever more demanding retailers—in its quest to grow.

Colgate is in the consumer-products business where market growth is roughly comparable to average GDP growth of 2 to 3 percent per year. Within these markets, Wal-Mart, Kmart, and CVS have become extraordinarily powerful retailers, dominating the sales of products in such areas as oral health care, baby and family care, beauty and home care.

Since Colgate is only roughly one-fifth the size of each of its primary competitors—Procter & Gamble and Unilever—it faces disadvantages of scale, size, and power in its relationships with the dominant discount retailers.

In its quest for revenue growth, the challenge for companies like Colgate is twofold. First is the fight for shelf space, convincing the Wal-Marts of this world that the consumers visiting their stores will prefer Colgate products. Second is developing the logistics and information-technology capability that provide the kind of delivery, speed, and service that will improve Wal-Mart's profitability for each square foot of shelf space it provides Colgate, which, of course, will encourage Wal-Mart to give Colgate even more space on its shelves.

Colgate has been very successful against both P&G and Unilever over the past two decades in the oral-care consumer-products market, and its success is a primary example of the kind of "good growth" and revenue productivity (a concept we will explore in detail in Chapter 5) that increases a company's stock price.

HOW GOOD GROWTH BUILDS VALUE

Obviously, growth of any kind increases revenues. Good growth, however, not only increases revenues but correspondingly improves profits and is sustainable over time. It is *primarily* organically (internally) generated from the ongoing operations and business of the company and is based on differentiated products and services that meet new or previously unmet consumer needs.

Good growth—that is, growth that is profitable, organic, differentiated, and sustainable—builds shareholder value over time. In contrast, bad growth destroys shareholder value. Mergers and acquisitions, a primary example of bad growth, are often based on myopic visions of synergy that have no basis in the reality of the marketplace. Instead of 4 plus 4 equaling 10, as promised when the deals are announced, more often than not 4 plus 4 winds up equaling 5 or 6. It is true that a large number of mergers and mega-acquisitions result in one-shot cost synergies—usually cost savings from the elimination of duplication with the merged enterprise—*but seldom in an improved rate of revenue growth that is sustainable for the long term.*

SearsRoebuck, for example, was the world's largest retailer in the early 1970s. It chose to accelerate its rate of growth through acquisitions, diluting its focus on retailing and broadening the base of its products and services to real estate (Century 21, Coldwell Banker), financial services (Dean Witter) and credit cards (Discover). It already had Allstate Insurance, which it had created in 1931. Sears' strategic premise was that the same customer base in retailing would buy these added services in a form of one-stop shopping. After some thirty years, Sears is all the way back to its core base of retailing, having divested all nonretailing operations, including Allstate. The last step in moving back to the future was announced in July 2003, when Sears said it was selling its entire credit and financial-products business to Citigroup for about $6 billion in cash. But in the interim, its position in the retail marketplace in the United States had gone backward, and it is now approximately one-eighth the size of Wal-Mart, which in 1970 was a small, regional retailer.

Compared with growing through a string of major acquisitions, good growth offers better returns over time, is less risky, and saves companies from crippling high debt and cash crises such as those faced by Vivendi and AOL Time Warner.

As Vivendi set about to transform itself from an obscure French water company to a global entertainment giant, its management went on an acquisition spree that would have made the most decorated "shopaholic" envious. In the United States alone, Vivendi acquired (among other things) Universal Studios, Blizzard Entertainment, and Def Jam. The problem? Vivendi overpaid and used debt to pay for most of those high-priced acquisitions. While the companies it bought were making money, Vivendi as a whole plunged into the red, after taking into account the repayment of interest on the billions of dollars it borrowed. The financial condition of the company became so acute that many wondered if it would survive. A new CEO was named who had no choice but to reduce debt. But that was not enough. Eventually the bulk of what is known as Vivendi Universal Entertainment—including all its entertainment components except music—was acquired by GE, which has been trying to broaden the base of its NBC division. The move makes excellent strategic sense for GE, which bought the assets at a very attractive price. It reduces dramatically NBC's dependence on traditional sources of advertising for its revenues from 90 percent to 45 percent.

Here's another example of bad growth. The heralded merger in 1998 of the number-two computer manufacturer Digital Equipment Corp. (DEC) with Compaq, then the world's largest personal-computer company, was a sheer disaster. In its attempt to be as broad as IBM in hardware and service, Compaq acquired Tandem before adding DEC. But then conditions in the market changed toward software and services, and the acquisitions were never properly digested and integrated into Compaq. As if that were not enough, the combined Compaq/Tandem/DEC merged with Hewlett-Packard just a few years later (the deal closed in 2002). The new giant is achieving cost synergies, but the jury is out in terms of how well it will do against Dell and IBM, which are growing both organically and by making strategic acquisitions to round out their product offerings.

By bringing up the examples of Sears, Vivendi, and Compaq, I am not universally condemning all acquisitions. There are times when scale (i.e., your overall size in relation to competitors) matters and it can be impossible to compete against industry giants without it. Phillips and Conoco were both relatively small fish in the energy market. They were both growing but they were at a huge competitive disadvantage versus ExxonMobil or BP. The Conoco-Phillips merger in 2002 (the new company is called ConocoPhillips) took out costs, and the integration of the two companies has been extremely successful. They have built on each other's strengths. Each has a particular expertise in searching for oil in different parts of the world, and the increased size of the combined company allows it to make larger exploration bets.

Similarly, there are times when an industry goes through a consolidation wave. At those moments, you either get bigger or find yourself at a disadvantage.

But overall, organic growth remains the way to go. It results in a better price-earnings ratio so that when an industry undergoes consolidation, this strength provides a company with the upper hand in making appropriate acquisitions against its competition. The end result is a company with additional scale and scope and greater credibility to go to the next level.

BAD GROWTH

Bad growth is not confined to mergers and acquisitions lacking strategic rationale. Price-cutting to gain market share without a corresponding decrease in costs can also lead to disaster.

One recent example took place in the building-materials industry, a business in which there are four major players, including one that we'll call Global Building Materials Inc. As is true of its competitors, Global Building is capital-intensive with high fixed costs and a high breakeven point.

Global Building's parent company brought in a new division head to run the business. He was the heir apparent to the CEO of the parent company and how he handled the new job would be a major test to see if he was ready for the top job.

The new manager believed that he could gain significant market share through cutting prices. He was successful—at least initially. Volume increased for the next two months, and Global Building's market share grew perceptibly.

However, the competition had no choice but to respond in kind, since a loss of market share in this high-fixed-cost industry means a loss of both cash flow and profitability. The end result of all that price cutting caused industry revenue and profits to shrink, which, obviously, affected Global Building as well.

The parent company had to revise its earnings estimates three times in the course of a year, and the stock price fell 60 percent. It took the succeeding division head two years to restore equilibrium to the business.

Global Building could have been successful in its effort to gain market share if the division head had improved productivity and offered higher-quality products and creating a better cost structure, ahead of the competition. With lower costs and higher-quality products, it would have been possible to cut prices and build market share while maintaining margin. Or he could have tried to search out the most profitable segments of the market and/or become the industry's innovator.

The problem with the course of action he chose was that there was no intrinsic competitive advantage. The only result was that everyone in the industry suffered. As always, there were personal consequences as well: The division head never did become a CEO.

BUYING GROWTH THROUGH
UNECONOMIC PRICE DISCOUNTING

Gaining market share by giving some customers unusually favorable credit terms—terms that result in your losing money on every sale—is another example of bad growth. It never works long term. Subsidizing buyers' purchases of your product by charging them little or no interest on the financing options you offer them, or by giving them an extended period until they have to pay you, may spike sales in the short term, but it is never effective as a long-term growth strategy.

We have seen the problems with this approach in countless cases, as manufacturers—especially in the telecom industry—gave their buyers ridiculously easy payment terms. They basically paid the financing costs their buyers would have been charged if they had to borrow to buy their product. The telecom companies put their own liquidity and credit rating at risk, thereby putting their entire company in jeopardy.

In these situations, companies are able to record revenues and profits in accounting terms, and managers get their bonuses for meeting targets, but at the end of the day a cash crisis arises and huge write-offs ensue.

GOOD GROWTH

The best companies, those that will thrive over the long run, grow both the top and bottom lines consistently over time, developing a cumulative competitive advantage that creates shareholder value. They may not turn in the best numbers in the industry when measured over any one short-term period, but their cumulative performance is stellar, thanks to the way they approach increasing their revenues. Their good growth also strengthens the company's DNA by creating new competencies and strengths, thereby building the skills of its people and confidence in the psyche of the organization.

What makes up good growth? It is profitable, organic, differentiated, and sustainable. Let's deal with these factors one at a time.

PROFITABLE

Good growth has to be not only profitable but capital-efficient—that is, it needs to earn a return on its investment greater than what the company could have received by putting its money in something ultra-safe, such as a Treasury bill. Colgate-Palmolive's growth is definitely profitable.

For more than a decade, Colgate has been on a sustained march to becoming number one in the oral-care consumer-products market, and, as mentioned, has edged out both Procter & Gamble and

Unilever. As important as its growth in revenues has been Colgate's steady improvement in profitability. Its gross margin has increased from 39 percent in 1984 to close to 60 percent in 2003, an improvement of almost one point per year.

Gross margin—your revenue less what it costs to make the product to obtain those revenues—is an important indicator of a company's profitability and often not given the due it deserves. Increasing gross margin and at the same time growing revenues at a rate better than the overall market is what makes for a great growth company. It is here that you can directly see the relationship between improved productivity and profitable growth. Colgate for more than a decade has been able to find ways to consistently enhance its competitive position by making its operations more productive and streamlining its processes.

The improvement of Colgate's gross margin also reflects its ability to innovate ahead of its two chief competitors. Colgate has created a corporate "growth group" with two major responsibilities. The first is to be continuously focused on developing new products, extending existing products, and improving packaging. The second, equally important, job is to concentrate on logistics, production, delivery, and speed and responsiveness to retailers through the effective use of data warehousing, information technology, and cost productivity. Again, it is an example of a top company recognizing that it must simultaneously improve productivity costs and grow.

Both processes resulted in Colgate's winning shelf space. It also meant lowering costs not only for Colgate but for retailers as well. Colgate reduced what it cost retailers to stock and sell its products while increasing retailers' inventory turns of Colgate products, thereby reducing the retailers' cost.

Colgate grew and grew more profitably than the competition, despite the huge lead that Procter & Gamble and Unilever had at the beginning of the race. It did so by continually focusing on the core business and finding ways to make it better. It emphasized "singles and doubles." Colgate obsessed about what was happening to its brands in each retail outlet, focused on the needs of retailers, created consumer awareness, continued to improve its products, and persuaded the consumer to prefer its products,

The growth path that Colgate chose has been good for shareholders and employees. The company's rapid growth has allowed it to attract the best managers in the industry—managers who are committed to growth.

ORGANIC

Organic growth in most cases has its genesis in the development and launch of ideas from within the organization.

Not only is it the most efficient way to create revenue growth—there are extremely important side benefits. It builds the creativity muscles of the organization and fosters team-building, since creating successful new products is, by definition, a multidisciplinary task. When people work with customers in the search for new ideas, translating those ideas into reality requires them to cut across silos and come together to make trade-offs and decisions in launching new products. It also builds the organization's self-confidence. Knowing that it has created a successful growth project makes it easier to tackle the next challenge, and the momentum feeds on itself.

Colgate's Total toothpaste was a natural result of the company's expertise and success in its core business of oral-care products. The toothpaste's patented formula provides twelve hours of protection against cavities, gingivitis, plaque, tartar buildup, and bad breath, while it whitens teeth. Offering all these benefits in one tube helped Colgate quickly gain market share—and, of course, increased the company's revenues in the process. But it was also a risk because Total incorporated an ingredient, triclosan, that needed Food and Drug Administration approval. (Triclosan helps reduce plaque and gingivitis.)

Designing a new product like Total requires research, formulation, development trials, and, in this case, final approval from the FDA. It has been a huge success, and Colgate's competition has not yet come up with anything comparable.

Organic growth can also be based on filling an additional customer need and/or exploiting an organization's existing expertise in products, customer segments, or geographic regions, to capture new markets. For example, Dell's move into servers storage and printers is an example of an adjacency, a product that fulfills a related need of the consumer.

While good growth is *primarily* organic, there are times when it makes sense to supplement organic growth with smaller "bolt-on" acquisitions to fill strategic gaps, such as gaining a beachhead in a geographic region, obtaining a new technology, filling an adjacent need, or adding a new distribution channel.

GE Medical Systems sells and services diagnostic machines (X-ray, MRI) to hospitals. A big unmet need for these hospital customers is to manage all of their patient information efficiently. GE Medical saw a big opportunity in digitizing hospitals but needed outside expertise in software and integrating this digitizing capability into its main business. Through a bolt-on acquisition of Marquette Electronics, GE medical acquired the skills and capabilities to create hospital information management as a profitable product line, one that is growing faster than medical spending as a whole.

DIFFERENTIATED

When someone talks about commoditization, what do you picture? That everyone competes on prices, and there is no differentiation?

That's the way most people see it. But if that were truly the case in the real world, then market share would be divided according to the production capacity of each of the participants every time companies competed to sell an equally priced product. That is almost never the case. Winners in the quest for profitable growth pay attention to differentiation, however razor-thin.

No matter how "commoditized" your business is, good-growth companies find a way to differentiate themselves. To do that, they see things through the eyes of their customers and potential customers, detect what these buyers prefer, and hook the customer through products, services, and relationships that are better differentiated than those of the competition.

You need look no further than Dell. At its heart, the company offers a commodity: personal computers. Yet Dell differentiated its product line by making sure its product was reliable, low-priced, and customizable—that is, customers can design their PCs exactly the way they want. This differentiation, coupled with Dell's continuous productivity improvements, focus on cost control and a supply chain that gives it the world's best inventory turns in the computer industry, allows the company to keep gaining market share in a slowing market.

At a more complex level, Lexus initially differentiated itself by positioning the car below Mercedes and above Cadillac, so customers were buying the prestige of a Mercedes but at a lower price.

However, where Lexus truly differentiated itself was in the postpurchase experience and in mechanical reliability. Year in and year out, Lexus owners report the fewest problems with their cars, and when there *is* a problem—even a perceived one—its dealers try to resolve it immediately. One Lexus owner told me that when he brought his car in for routine maintenance, he mentioned in passing that the car's automatic transmission seemed a bit sluggish. It took a bit longer than he expected for the engine to shift gears. He was *not* complaining, he told his service adviser—just passing along a quirk he found in the car he otherwise loved.

Service technicians checked out the car and agreed that the car was shifting gears slowly, but they could not find a cause. Lexus' solution? The company replaced the transmission—a $7,000 job—at no cost to the customer.

Lexus could afford to take this step because its dealers sell a profitable product that results in few complaints from customers. The Lexus is a good value for the buyer, and the driving and maintenance experience is nearly worry-free.

What the Lexus and Dell examples make clear is that customers can discern differences when the price of competing products is exactly the same, through better delivery, better emotional appeal, or better post-purchase experience.

Differentiation can also take place in the service that a manufacturer provides to retailers like Wal-Mart. In this case, differentiation takes place through the use of logistics—synchronization of the manufacturer's marketing programs with the retailer and helping the retailer achieve its aspiration of providing products and services in a way that is unique to each of its regions. For example, a supplier could help Wal-Mart design specific programs to spur sales to Hispanics.

By helping the customer increase its sales, the manufacturer has differentiated itself from being just another firm that the customer does business with.

SUSTAINABLE

Good growth continues over time. It has a sustainable trajectory. You are *not* looking for a quick spike upward in revenues, caused by cutting prices or by throwing substantial resources against a one-shot opportunity. The goal is to have the growth continue year after year. For example, the growth of Southwest Airlines has been based on a consistent set of actions. New routes are carefully vetted—the goal is to have them be profitable in less than a year—and turnaround times (the period from when a plane pulls into a gate until it pushes back on another flight) are substantially faster than the industry average, allowing Southwest planes to fly more trips a day than its competitors.

If you look at one of the suppliers to the airline industry, you can see another example of sustainable growth. In this case, the move toward sustainability was prompted out of necessity.

When the airline industry declined in the early 1990s, it led to a decrease in the revenues of firms that sold aircraft engines. GE Aircraft Engines redefined the needs of its airline customers to include not just the engines themselves but also servicing them on a regular basis. Up to that point, a major airline would use the service shop of one company in, say, Chicago and that of completely different companies in its other locations around the world. Some also did the service themselves in their own shops.

GE's new value proposition was to provide total service around the globe. Through innovation, use of information technology, and managerial ability to provide better maintenance, the result would be less downtime for the airlines and lower costs. For example, doing a major overhaul on its own might have required an airline to fly its plane back empty to its service facility. With service operations around the world, GE can do the work wherever a plane is, which gets the plane back in the air, generating revenues sooner. And because it specializes, GE can do the necessary service work faster, increasing productivity for the airlines once again. Scores of airlines took advantage of the chance to outsource the maintenance part of their business to a single supplier.

Before its chief competitor, Pratt & Whitney, woke up, GE Aircraft Engines captured 70 percent of the airplane-service market. And, of course, the service contracts tied customers more closely to GE, giving it a leg up in selling the core product—engines—and developing a sustained trajectory of growth by having a built-in revenue stream, the money that comes in month in and month out from the service contracts.

In this case, the "single" and "double" of adding a service component to a product created a platform that is a home run in terms of a sustained, decades-long trajectory of growth. The recurring revenues from the service work are extremely reliable. Not only has GE Aircraft Engines outgrown the competition—its model of adding service to products became a best practice for other GE businesses, which are now adding higher-margin service work into their product mix.

It is also an example of building both scale and scope and then learning how to leverage for growth. GE Aircraft's number-one position in the marketplace, combined with organic growth and simultaneous productivity, gave it the leverage to make acquisitions in the service area.

But the only way this growth is going to occur is if everyone in the organization believes it to be possible. It is up to the organization's leadership to create the right mind-set.

4

Leadership for Growth:
Confronting the Enemy Within

Every leader—those in charge of individual products, the heads of business units, the CEO—needs a growth agenda and the ability to communicate an urgency about the need to increase revenues and build the business. They need to do this so that action-oriented people within the organization find out what needs to be done *today* to help the company become better tomorrow.

Without this leadership, the organization stagnates, and its employees get frustrated. It's the reason why Bill Carter, the manager of the Furniture Globe store discussed in Chapter 1, threw down his copy of the *Wall Street Journal*, sighed, and got up and stared out the window over the kitchen sink.

His first thought was a sarcastic, "It was sure nice of them to tell us ahead of time," and then, feeling betrayed, he started to figure out how he was going to break the news to the people in his store, and wondered whether word would have reached them before he got into the office. (It probably would have. When it came to bad news, the grapevine was remarkably efficient.)

The problem was simple. Carter's new boss, Dave Duncan, executive vice president of the conglomerate that had acquired Furniture Globe, had told the *Journal* that the company was about to launch its third round of "major cost-cutting" in less than two years because "there just isn't any growth in the furniture market. The entire segment is flat."

Duncan's assessment that "we're a mature business, and growth is slowing because population growth and personal income are flat" made Carter madder than hell. Every day he saw the growth in the upwardly mobile Hispanic community in Miami, the part of the market his store serves.

Maybe the overall industry was flat, but the Miami Hispanic community is a distinct segment that Carter knew he could grow significantly. If corporate could just give him a few more resources, or simply let him once again have some discretion to source items of interest to sell to his customers, he knew he could get additional revenues.

What was left unsaid in the *Journal* article was that the bonuses of Duncan and other people in corporate headquarters are tied only to improvement in margins and cash flow, something relatively easy to achieve through quarter-by-quarter cost control and improving cash flow by reducing inventory. How the bonuses are determined drove behavior from the CEO right down the chain of command.

It seemed to Carter that Duncan was saying that "growth is beyond our control," and that senior management was creating a self-fulfilling prophecy. Once you start down that path, Carter thought, sooner or later you will turn just about all your attention to cost-cutting, and that was already the number-one topic when he went to regional meetings. Some 90 percent of the time at those two-day affairs was spent talking about how to reduce inventory substantially and cut labor costs by getting by with more part-time people, and how the slashing of the local advertising budget was no big deal.

The context and tone of those quarterly meetings have changed dramatically, thought Carter. "We used to talk about how the customers' needs were changing, what new merchandise looked promising, whether there were better ways to display what we have to sell, and how we could reward our best salespeople," he explained when his wife asked him what had gotten him so upset. "Those meetings used to be all about getting more sales. We were obsessed with it. If we had a chance to boost our prices, we deliberately wouldn't. We figured—correctly—that keeping our prices low would bring even more customers into the stores. Now all we talk about is cash, costs, and doing more with less."

That kind of mind-set, Carter intuitively knew, has never led to the creation of a dynamic company over the long term.

"Why don't they get it?" his wife asked him.

"It is a great question," he said. "Maybe we've met the enemy and they are us."

BECOMING A REVENUE GROWTH LEADER

Of course, the leader of the corporation or the business unit determines the strategy, positions the business, ensures customer needs are fulfilled, and develops and inspires people. But if she is not connected to growth projects, as well as productivity *and* linking them together, then, indeed, "the enemy is us."

When we are discussing the leader's role, it is easy to assume that we are focusing on the CEO. And clearly she is a major factor, since she will have a big impact on the corporate mind-set. But by *leader* we are also talking about the heads of the individual business units, the person in charge of individual products or functions such as marketing and logistics and leaders of cross-functional teams.

Every leader must be truly committed to growth. Part of the job is to "walk the talk," to act as if growth is important and to constantly communicate its urgency. That includes consistently getting information and intelligence about customers' needs directly, unfiltered by the corporate hierarchy and communicating this information to all in her area of responsibility.

This is something Sam Walton did throughout his life. He constantly visited the stores, and he did more than just walk up and down the aisles. He talked to Wal-Mart "associates" to discover what was selling and what wasn't and what customers were asking for that the stores didn't have; he talked to management, of course, but he also spent time with customers and suppliers and walked around competitors' stores (often getting thrown out, once he was recognized).

Walton (and his successors have followed the same practices) was trying to gain unfiltered information about what was going on. Just about every question he asked, and almost every action he took, was designed to figure out how to keep his customers coming back (so that they would buy more) or was designed to discover what Wal-Mart could do to increase its sales.

And Walton didn't stop there. He set up a social system to ensure that his thirty regional managers did the same. Every week, each visited nine stores of their own and six of the competition. They would meet, along with people from merchandising, advertising, finance, and logistics, to discuss what they learned about the competition, customers, merchandise, what was selling and not selling, and what was out of stock. They resolved conflicts then and there and made decisions about what could be done to spark sales.

SPREADING THE WORD

Once customer information is gathered, it then has to be communicated internally, and then followed up to make sure that it is used to develop and foster the growth agenda.

For example, at Columbus, Ohio–based Sterling Commerce, a leading global provider of e-business software and service solutions, the president and CEO, Samuel R. Starr, holds a company-wide meeting of all senior people every Monday morning between 9 and 10. (Those who cannot be physically present at headquarters participate via conference call.) The sole purpose of the meeting: revenue growth. The discussion centers on what projects are in the pipeline, what Sterling is doing to get a bigger share of the customer's wallet, and what new products the company should be offering.

These meetings solve a common problem. "Before, the management team never had the best intelligence about customers and competitors," says Starr, whose company is a wholly owned subsidiary of SBC Communications. "What was going on in the company was filtered up through several layers, and people were often afraid to report when they were having problems. As a result, we would be expecting to book revenues on deals that were in trouble, a fact that we didn't realize until it was too late and the deal was gone.

"Now, we work off a real-time agenda," says Sterling. "If there is a problem closing a deal—say, that the legal department and our sales force have been having trouble getting together on terms—we talk right then and there about not only what the problem is but exactly how we are going to solve it and when, and people report back at the next meeting. We get real information in real time. As a result of having everyone together, I learn directly what needs to be done, and not just what people want me to hear. There is accountability, and because all the senior people are present, the walls between the departments are eliminated." Sterling Commerce is closing deals far faster than ever before. When people see that the leader is demanding, receiving, and acting on this kind of information flow, they know he is serious about growth.

Sam Starr and his people experienced new energy by increasing revenues and shortening the amount of time it took to close deals. Those increased revenues were achieved without increasing costs. The weekly rhythm of the social process they developed synchronized the alignment and priorities of nonsales functions such as finance, legal, and product development. The process made them individually and collectively customer-centric.

ACTIONS DO SPEAK LOUDER THAN WORDS

Companies focused entirely on costs and productivity are beginning to face the fact that they need to grow as well. David Cote, the newly appointed CEO of Honeywell International, has made the linkage of growth and productivity a major part of his leadership platform, asking every leader to devote 30 percent of his time to revenue growth. To underscore the message, Cote is making growth the key subject at all senior management meetings. Every six to eight weeks, senior managers now attend a meeting devoted solely to growth—and both they and Cote are regularly calling on customers.

It has become fashionable to say, "I have made a customer call." But when the best leaders visit a customer, they make sure they know what opportunities and threats the customer is facing. They don't have to waste any time at the meeting being educated about their customer's industry conditions. The leader is there to talk, one-on-one, and offer whatever help he can. Yes, of course, they use the meeting to resolve whatever problems may exist, but the real purpose is to look for ways to help the customer grow his revenues. Over time, this approach will help you discover opportunities for your own revenue growth.

THE TYRANNY OF SELF-FULFILLING PROPHECIES

Every organization (including yours?) that has experienced a problem growing revenues has tried to explain away why the lack of growth wasn't its fault. The arguments are often based on conventional wisdom within a company or an industry as a whole. And it may be true that a company—or indeed an entire sector, or even the entire country—is in a slump, but that does not mean there are no growth opportunities.

Total sales in your industry may have been $30 billion last year, and let's assume that they are going to be $30 billion this year. But why are you comparing yourself to the average? In every industry there are segments that are growing and declining. The question, of course, is whether you can move into those segments that are growing. Investigate how other players in your industry are managing to increase revenues. What are they doing to segment and re-segment the industry from different angles? What are they seeing that you are not? (We will talk much more about segmenting in Chapter 7.)

When senior management believes that there is no growth, rationalizing that "we're in a mature industry," the self-fulfilling prophecy starts to take over.

When you hear people saying things like, "No company in the furniture industry [for example] is growing," they engage in psychological distortion. People see what they want to see, searching for an excuse that explains away the inability to increase revenues. For example, Bill Carter's boss, Dave Duncan, clearly ignored the fact that other specialty retailers are indeed growing, and that there is substantial growth in the Southeast.

People in Detroit often say that growth in the automobile business is anemic, yet Toyota continues to gain profitable market share almost every year in the United States. It is always a sure tip-off that someone is trying to explain away the problem when he talks in generalities ("no one is growing") rather than engaging in specifics.

Companies that are dominant in their industry may try to justify lack of revenue growth by saying, "We're so big that there is nowhere else for us to grow." That usually is not the case. As Larry Bossidy, the former CEO of Honeywell International, said, "No market is ever fully penetrated." You can always segment and re-segment to find more opportunities. You can also broaden the scope of the market need you serve to gain a larger share of customer's wallet, as we showed in the Coke–Pepsi battle in the non-cola market.

HOW TO DEAL WITH RISK

When I speak with middle managers, I often hear them express frustration that the people above them don't know how to take risks. They are all risk-averse is the common complaint.

Risk is inherent when you try to do anything new, and by definition trying to increase revenue calls for new ways of thinking. People often do not properly assess the potential rewards for taking a risk. Nor do they focus on how well the risks and rewards match.

Suppose you discover that a potential growth initiative offers both high risk and high reward? Then, you ask the next question: "If we take this high risk and we fail, will we lose the ranch?" You may not want to go ahead if the answer is yes—but you might; sometimes it *is* worth betting the company on a new idea—but you always want to have a handle on what you are up against. You also want to know how to reduce risk, shape it, and manage it.

If the risk is not of the bet-the-company type, you then ask, "If we fail, will it put us at a severe competitive disadvantage?" If not, you dig a bit deeper and try to figure just how badly the organization will be hurt if the idea doesn't work.

Convinced the risk is worth taking, you then drill down farther and decide whether the project is too risky, given the other risks in your company's investment portfolio, and decide whether the inclusion of this project will push the company over the edge. Should you still decide to take the risk ahead, you can ask whether sharing the risk by an alliance would be an acceptable option.

For example, Warner Lambert bet its survival on the cholesterol drug Lipitor. There is no guarantee that any drug will make money. The pharmaceutical companies do not know if the discovery will receive FDA approval. And even if it does, there is no certainty it will repay the investment required to discover and produce it. Top management decided to reduce the risk by sharing it with Pfizer. In exchange for $250 million and getting additional vast sales coverage following the launch of the drug, Warner Lambert shared a percentage of the forthcoming profits with Pfizer. No one had expected Lipitor to be one of the biggest blockbuster drugs of all time. It was such a success that the stock price of Warner Lambert quadrupled before the company's eventual acquisition by Pfizer.

THE HINGE ASSUMPTION

Once you have a good understanding of the risk/reward ratio, you get to the most critical question of all, one designed to get at what I call the "hinge assumption." You ask: "What is the one assumption we are making that could cause the whole project to fail if it turns out to be wrong." By asking this question, you are trying to discover the one supposition that you have made that is central to everything else.

The hinge assumption could be an external one. For example, "We have proven technology that the customers want and will buy. But if they don't, we are doomed." Iridium was a telecommunications venture involving seventy-seven satellites, conceived, shaped, and launched by TRW, Motorola, and Boeing. Iridium's Celestial Satellite Network assumed that consumers would want and pay for a cell phone that worked anywhere in the world. Success depended on three hinge assumptions. The first was that "the dog would eat the dog food," that is, that the quality and price of the phone would be what customers wanted. Second, that there would be enough customers on a worldwide basis. And third, that all the requisite governments would approve the licenses. While they got the necessary regulatory approvals, the first two hinges broke. Write-offs for the companies involved came to hundreds of millions of dollars, and the venture is almost on its deathbed.

The hinge assumption can be huge: "We *know* consumers want X"—or it can be incredibly small—"Fred is the key to this whole initiative; if he dies or goes to a competitor, the project fails." But no matter what it is, there is always one key assumption. You have to determine what it is, and you must decide if you have that specific risk under control.

The skill of risk evaluation definitely needs to be worked on if your people are not taking risks. And it certainly needs to be in place before employees start making pie-in-the-sky projections such as Iridium's.

Risk evaluation is hard work and requires looking at the market from the outside-in, asking: What is the risk in the marketplace? What are the risks we can't control? Without the outside-in approach, you will have a hell of a time growing the business.

People also have problems dealing with risk because their leaders may be sending the wrong message. This could be the case if you overhear people within your organization say such things as, "The guy at the top doesn't want us to take chances."

They could reach this conclusion by paying attention to all the questions you ask when someone brings up a new idea. You know you are just drilling down to figure out where the potential landmines are when you ask about market risks, hinge assumptions, and the like. But *they* may not. You know you are just doing your home-work. But people within your organization may add up the questions you are asking and conclude that you think the initiative they are proposing is too risky.

And if you go through the same due diligence—and you should—by asking all these questions about potential risks and rewards, every time someone proposes a new idea, your people could con-clude that you think *all* initiatives are too risky.

You have to make it clear—every time—why you are asking the questions.

The final reason your organization may have problems with risk? Your people may not have the skills to handle fluid situations, so they do everything in their power to avoid them. It takes a certain mind-set and comfort level to deal successfully with risk.

That is something that soldiers have long understood. At every military academy, they teach, "The battle plan is the first casualty of war." The aphorism means that once the fighting starts, it is almost certain to evolve in a way that no one could foresee.

The same thing holds true in business. As your company moves into a new area, it is likely the situation won't unfold the way you drew it up. If your people are uncomfortable with that, they will avoid trying anything new. If that is the case, you probably have to change your people.

But if you have the right people, people who have the right mind-set, there are specific tools you can use to produce profitable growth. Let's turn to them next.

5

Accelerating Profitable Revenue Growth Through Revenue Productivity

The basic need of most businesses today is accelerating revenue growth initiatives through singles and doubles. That quest is aided by revenue productivity, a tool that shows how to grow revenues without using a disproportionate amount of resources. The tool of revenue productivity turns thought and action from cost-cutting to revenue growth by analyzing everything a business does from mundane day-to-day tasks to the vitally important. In effect, it turns your thinking about productivity on its head, as we'll illustrate with the recent experience of a Chicago-based medical products company.

After a long famine, it introduced a flood of innovative products into the marketplace. Revenues, however, did not increase. The head of sales asked for more resources to better enable his staff to sell more of the new product. He did not get them. As is true at most companies, quarter-by-quarter budgeting pressure and the demands from Wall Street for bottom-line performance made it hesitant about pouring more resources into the sales function. But, there was also a more fundamental question that kept the sales force from receiving more money. Jim, the CEO of the company, was wondering whether it was a matter of insufficient resources or the quality of the sales force and the way it was deployed that was holding sales back. The question was very much on Jim's mind when I went out to dinner with him, his wife, Linda, and Bill, the COO of the company.

Early in the week, Jim's secretary reserved a table for us at what was being heralded as *the* place to eat in Chicago.

Now, the only thing Jim enjoys almost as much as his family and running his company is rooting for the Chicago Bears of the National Football League. That Saturday, Jim got caught up watching the NFL draft, and we didn't pull up at the front door of the restaurant until 8:13. By the time the valet came for the car and we had made our way to the hostess stand, it was slightly after 8:15.

"Reservation for four," Jim said, giving his name. As the hostess looked in her book, Jim waved to a couple of people he knew and noticed that a few people he didn't know were staring at him. That had begun happening recently, since he started to become a regular on covers of business magazines.

"I am sorry, sir," the hostess began, not sounding sorry at all. "We gave away your reservation."

"You *what?*"

"It was for 8 o'clock, and it is," she paused to make it a point to look at her watch, "8:20 now.

"As you can see, we are packed, and I just couldn't hold the table for you any longer. If you'd like to wait at the bar, I think something might open up around 10:00."

We certainly did not like seeing our reservation disappear, but it was less *what* the hostess said than *how* she said it. Her attitude was indifferent and uncaring, not even bothering to see if there was a way to find a table to accommodate us.

Incredulous, Jim told us that he knew a better spot, a restaurant he visited no more than once or twice a year. It, too, was crowded.

"I am sorry, but we don't have a reservation," Jim told the hostess.

"No problem," she said. "Give me a minute." She tracked down two busboys, who carried a table for four to the back of the bar area, and within three minutes we were seated in a space that looked for all the world as if it had been waiting for us.

Still fuming from his distasteful interaction with the first hostess, Jim had a sudden realization as he started in on his second drink. Maybe what he had just experienced at the first restaurant could explain the revenue growth problems at his own company. Maybe his salespeople, just like the hostess, were limiting profitable revenue growth. His marketing and R&D people were coming up with new innovative products, but sales were not growing correspondingly. The more he thought about it, the more he could see the same sort of arrogance and attitude ("We're the best; we have the largest market share") among his sales force that he could see in the first hostess ("We are full; you are late; it is your fault.").

LOOKING DIFFERENTLY AT PRODUCTIVITY

Traditional cost productivity is almost always about reducing expenses. Revenue productivity, on the other hand, increases revenues from the same level of cost. Alternatively, one can increase revenues dramatically without increasing expenses on a proportionate level. Increasing revenue productivity provides the foundation for investing more resources to further growth.

Revenue productivity involves analyzing everything a business does every day, from simple actions like how the call center of a business works, for example, or how a hostess treats guests at a restaurant to the obviously important. Some examples of the latter include examining the revenue-generating effectiveness of the sales force and its sales management, logistics, pricing structure, and the social system of product launches to obtain profitable *peak market share* faster.

Revenue productivity requires a different psychology. For example, the mind-set of the call center changes from how many more calls can be handled—which means "how fast can we get a caller off the phone"—in a day to one in which the tone of the representative makes the customer feel that she is welcome and that issues will be satisfactorily resolved. It converts the customer from a potential complainer to someone who spreads positive word of mouth, and someone who is likely to buy again in the future.

The discussion among myself, Jim, Linda, and Bill about the implications of the behavior of the hostess at the first restaurant continued through dinner and on into the following day. Jim came to realize that, in his own case, revenue growth had little to do with the amount of resources expended on the sales force. Given its quality, composition, and the way it was managed, additional money really wouldn't help. Jim, however, was psychologically blocked about confronting the issue. Many of the salespeople had been with him since the company's founding more than twenty years ago.

To help Jim think through the issue of how effective his sales force is at revenue generation, I asked him on a scale of one to ten (with ten being best) how he would rate the quality of match between the requirements for selling the new products and the current skills of the sales force. Jim answered that "about 15 percent are a superb match. They are superstars—high 9s or 10s. About 35 percent are probably 2s or 3s. Their skills are obsolete in the context of the new game in which a new form of selling and building relationships is required. The remainder are in between the superstars and lower performers, and I would rate them about a 5."

I then told Jim that he had to be intellectually honest about whether those rated as "5s" had the potential to substantially increase revenues if they received training and coaching. I then asked Jim about compensation and he said that "the superstars are making about $250,000. From there the compensation falls. The lowest paid salespeople make about $100,000." Then Jim was struck by the obvious. The salesperson earning $250,000 was a different breed. He and Bill, the COO, had been hesitant about replacing the poor performers with superstars because they had been thinking in traditional ways of cost management, especially given the bind they were in with new products not selling to expectation. They had wanted to keep expenses to a minimum.

A commitment to increasing costs to grow revenues always causes a level of uncertainty. That was especially true for Bill, the COO, who came from a manufacturing background where he watched every penny and dramatically improved the company's cost position. Finding the right additional "superstars" in a reasonable amount of time and assimilating them properly were other sources of uncertainty. The fact that Jim had a long history with many of the 2s and 3s also added to his angst. They had helped him grow the business in the past and he felt indebted to them. Despite the uncertainty, Jim made the decision to move forward. His first step was a change in sales management. They, in turn, have revamped the quality, composition, and organization of the sales staff so that it is in sync with the new realities. The change in the mix of skills of the sales staff and their more effective deployment are now driving the growth in revenue.

While absolute costs are increasing with the addition of more highly compensated superstars, the growth in revenues has more than compensated for the increased expense.

A restaurant hostess with the wrong attitude about customers results in negative revenue productivity. Magnify that several times over with a sales force that becomes demoralized because across-the-board cost-cutting results in larger territories and too many products to sell. Cost goals are achieved, but the end result is a disproportionate reduction in revenues, profits, and market share.

Suppose the sales force generates $250 million in revenues and the salespeople themselves cost $50 million annually, once all costs (salary, commissions, bonuses, and health insurance) are taken into account. On top of that, we'll assume that another $20 million is spent on supervision and support.

In trying to increase productivity, the typical first reaction is to cut costs. Maybe you could get these same $250 million in sales with only $65 million in costs, by cutting some salespeople and expanding the territories of others. You would have saved $5 million, but the company would not have grown at all. Perhaps worse, the odds are small that another $5 million could be taken out next year.

In contrast, revenue productivity starts with the question: Can we increase our profitable sales? In the case of the sales force, for example, is there a way to take some of the $20 million spent on support and allocate that money differently, giving, say, assistants to the reps to handle paperwork and thereby enabling them to increase the number of sales calls? Or are there prospecting techniques such as state-of-the-art sales lists and better directories of sales leads to search out more qualified prospects?

Bob Whitman, the CEO of Franklin Covey, and his team are working with several leading pharmaceutical companies. Members of the industry-leading sales force made, on average, 570 face-to-face sales calls on doctors a year, while another leading company, which was anxious to increase its revenue, made more than 20 percent fewer calls.

Why the discrepancy? Well, for one thing, although the second company thought it made increasing the number of face-to-face calls on doctors a priority, you couldn't prove it by a survey of the sales force. They reported that increasing calls on doctors was just one of a number of things the company told them to concentrate on. In fact, less than 15 percent identified it as a top personal priority.

But even when they want to increase their calls, the salesmen said they were bogged down in paperwork, had too wide an area to cover, and had less than a distinctive value proposition to offer doctors. While the leading pharmaceutical company could offer physicians everything from state-of-the-art clinical results on the drugs they were selling to ways to increase the profitability of their practice, salesmen at the second company had no such resources at their disposal.

Armed with these findings, the second drug company resized the sales territories, beefed up the help it gave the sales force, and made clear to the reps that increasing the number of sales calls is their number-one priority. While the changes have been in place for a short amount of time, the effects are already noticeable. The number of sales calls per day is climbing and at this level, when rolled out throughout the company, the increase in revenue should top one billion dollars annually. More important, from a competitive positioning viewpoint, it will improve the market share of this already leading drug company.

Another major factor for revenue productivity and revenue generation, given the increasing complexity of most business-to-business selling, is the configuration of the sales force. Should it be geographically focused or organized by customer (industry) segments? The former is almost always based on cost productivity, the latter on revenue productivity. Organizing by customer segment is almost always higher in cost, but the payoff can be worth it.

As a company's offerings become more complex and its customer mix and niche players become stronger, there comes a time when you seriously need to evaluate organizing your sales force by customer segment. Louis Gerstner used this approach to help turn IBM around. Having been a customer of IBM's when he was CEO of American Express, Gerstner knew a salesperson cannot truly understand the problems and opportunities in more than one industry, especially when he has to do solutions selling. Today's customers demand that the salesperson know the industry well enough to bring them relevant, innovative ideas. The sales force, therefore, needs to specialize. In IBM's case, that meant Gerstner actively reconfigured it to serve specific industries, such as financial services or telecommunications.

Organizing the sales force by industry is not just the province of Fortune 100 companies like IBM. NDC Health, the Atlanta-based health information services company, organized its sales force in accordance with its four customer segments: physicians, pharmacies, hospitals, and pharmaceutical companies. We will see the results a little later.

A DIFFERENT MIND-SET

What is clear is that obtaining revenue productivity requires a different corporate mind-set, one that is quite different from cost productivity alone. Here, what you spend is less important than what you spend it on and the revenue it produces. And just as you get everyone to focus on cost-cutting, you need to get everyone focused on revenue productivity.

When revenue starts to dry up, there is an established mind-set that says, "We need to face facts." The thinking becomes: Without more coming in on the top line, we must make do with what we have—and perhaps even less. The tendency is to cut, and often the cuts are made in the most crucial areas—people who have direct contact with customers, employees who can discover unmet market needs.

The managers making those cuts frequently justify those moves by saying that they are just trying to maintain the company's return on investment (ROI). But they fail to see an alternative.

A company's ROI is nothing more than a ratio: how much a company makes, divided by how much it spends. The formula looks like this:

$$R(eturn) \ O(n) \ I(nvestment) = Earnings/Investment$$

The cost-cutters try to boost that number by reducing the denominator, how much they invest. But you can get the same result by keeping the investment the same and increasing how much you earn. That simple change in focus is what revenue productivity is all about.

When someone commits to *cost* productivity—that is, he is going to cut expenses in order to increase net income—the outcome is deterministic ("We will cut costs") and certain. You know when you are finished. You are done when X percent of costs have been removed from the budget.

When you commit to *revenue* productivity, it is less of a sure thing. And that issue can concern some people. It certainly concerned the people who work for Jim when they learned about his plan to revamp sales management and hire superstar salespeople.

When the argument was made that Jim should replace most of his sales force with "tens," people who commanded $250,000 a year, one senior manager was hesitant. She asked how the company could be sure that all of these expensive new people are going to produce. The answer obviously is that there are no guarantees. However, managers are paid to define what needs to be done and then to make sure that what needs to be done *gets* done. In this case, many of the salespeople did not have the skills required to sell the new product line and the job of management is to confront the issue.

Much of this chapter has been devoted to using the example of how the sales force of a business can enhance revenue productivity. But the usefulness of the tool extends to every part of the business. For example, people managing the logistics system for a retailer have an important role to play in ensuring that it never runs out of a popular product. If you don't have the right merchandise when the customer wants it, you (obviously) cannot sell it to her. And odds are that she won't come back and the sale is lost.

Managers responsible for launching products can focus on the time for achieving profitable peak market share. For example, the success or failure of mass-market blockbuster movies rests less with how quickly they can be produced and launched ("time to market") than with how well they do during their first weekend in theaters. Revenue productivity requires film studios to make huge investments in advertising and publicity to make sure the movie "opens big," that it generates substantial revenues during the first few days it is available for viewing. Time to peak market share generates the best revenues, profits, and cash flow. It forces you to think about timing the launch so that you come to market at a time and in a space that makes you less vulnerable to the competition.

But revenue productivity doesn't have to be anything as dramatic as the opening of the new *Terminator* or *Matrix* movie. It can be as simple as a hotel clerk reminding a guest that two-hour dry cleaning is available. And revenue productivity can be as basic as asking a repairman out on a call to glance around the customer's home to see what other appliances might need servicing or should be replaced (and making sure he communicates that information to the right department).

Revenue productivity is imperative for every business, but it's an absolute necessity for those with low margins and high fixed-cost structures, such as the auto business. If a company like GM focuses only on cost reduction without generating additional revenue, not enough falls to the bottom line, the result being that there are not enough resources to refresh the product line.

LET'S REVIEW

Revenue productivity, just like overall revenue growth, begins with the understanding that getting more sales is everyone's job. Here, though, thinking differently is required. Traditionally, managers look to cut costs to increase earnings. With revenue productivity, costs remain the same but revenues increase significantly. When the level of cost actually rises, the level of revenues increases proportionately more.

Revenue productivity is imperative and everyone can contribute. Leadership needs to stress it, talk about it daily, and department heads must follow through. The growth budget, the concept we will discuss next, can be a big help in that regard.

6

Building a Growth Budget

E VERYONE IN BUSINESS wants profitable revenue growth. But few managers have an explicit handle on what (if anything) they are spending to obtain it. Knowing the percentage of revenues your company spends today to build revenues for the short (this year), medium (two to five years out), and long (five years or more) terms is the basis for the concept of the growth budget. This new idea I developed while working with my clients is a dedicated way of funding growth by providing the discipline, the process, and the follow-through to make it a reality. It's also an effective tool for allocating resources to make tradeoffs between the short-term and long-term.

Companies are composed of silos—the marketing department, manufacturing and operations, research and development, sales, and so on—which often are not effectively linked together to obtain revenue growth. As the CEO of a financial-services company recently told me, each of his product-line managers (for example, the people who design and develop products such as mutual funds) and the managers of distribution channels (the people who sell their mutual funds to consumers and institutional investors) plan growth on their own, despite the fact that they need and depend on one another to develop and sell products and thereby grow the business. While the manager developing new equity offerings needs the person running the retail distribution channel to sell her products to customers, they each go their own way when it comes time to try to increase revenues. Sometimes, by chance, parts of the various plans mesh. But often they do not.

The growth budget is the vehicle for overcoming this obstacle. It links these silos and gets managers to collaborate. Creating a growth budget forces managers to discuss both the priorities of their individual departments and the organization-wide resources devoted to revenue growth and then make trade-offs to determine the combined priorities and mix of resources for getting better revenue growth. It is a different—and more effective—way to determine how a company is going to fund the growth it needs.

Most companies have a disciplined budgeting process that requires a commitment with regard to revenues, costs, profits, and cash flow. The most common budget item that relates to growth is research and development, and, like almost 95 percent of items in the budget, it is regarded as a cost item. Growth, however, requires costs to be incurred in more than just R&D. And, almost always, these resources for growth are scattered throughout the budget. Worse, they are not tied to generating revenues within any specific time horizon.

Let's say that a software company wants to invest significant money in a study on how the market is changing, or commit resources to refurbish the sales force so that it has the capability to do solutions selling instead of just moving individual pieces of software. Or suppose a consumer-products company wants to invest in a new logistical system and IT architecture to keep track of thousands of individual stock-keeping units (SKUs) to improve customer inventory turns and cash flow. They're all key investments for medium- and long-term growth, but the financial resources to make them happen are scattered in department budgets throughout the company. By bringing them together in a growth budget, the company can make a disciplined, focused commitment to spend resources to grow the business. Growth budgets are an easy way to track your organization's investment in the future. After all, you are spending money from the growth budget on projects designed to increase future revenues through new products or services.

The growth budget is a plan that lays out not only how the organization intends to find growth, but how it proposes to fund that quest. It should be made transparent to everyone in the organization, so that each employee knows there is a serious ongoing commitment to find additional revenues.

This commitment will speak more loudly than anything a leader might say about what will attract his energy and attention and what will not. It tells everyone in the organization what he thinks is important (and, implicitly, what he thinks is not). The growth budget explains how the leader will fund those projects and those ideas that are designed to increase revenues.

The growth budget should be audited for quality and execution and be reviewed with the same intensity as costs. If $1 million is spent on upgrading the sales force, then you need to measure if that expenditure increases revenues and margins in a disciplined, planned way.

THE GROWTH BUDGET AND THE BIG "AH-HA"

The usefulness of a growth budget recently hit home with Randy Jones, the president of a $5 billion division of a Fortune 100 company, during a mid-year budget review meeting. When the meeting shifted to a discussion of growth and the plans for increasing revenues, Jones asked his nine direct reports what they each thought the division would spend in the current fiscal year regardless of whether the growth would happen over the short, medium, or long terms. The answers ranged from $30 to $100 million, with everyone conceding that the answer he gave was pure guesswork.

Jones was shocked at the answers, since the real number was $200 million. He realized that one reason the division was having difficulty growing, despite the amount of money spent, was lack of a process that explicitly identified and prioritized the resources devoted to growth. In fact, several of the people at the meeting had been complaining that the division had not been investing enough in growth projects.

Jones could see that all of the resources devoted to growth were scattered across different cost center functions and departments of the division. The traditional budget did not make this number transparent. Nor did it reveal the linkage between costs incurred and revenues expected on either a short-term or long-term basis. He announced an unscheduled one-hour break in the meeting while he and the division CFO pulled all of the numbers related to growth that were part of the budget.

When the meeting reconvened, he specifically showed how the division was spending $200 million for growth:

- Research in basic technologies for long-term growth scattered through the various departments: $50 million

- Improvement of IT infrastructure to create logistics systems and data warehouses better focused on the customer: $60 million
- Product development and product extensions: $70 million
- Sales force training and development for solutions selling: $10 million
- Creating a new unit for customer segmentation and consumer research: $10 million

Jones and his team came to the conclusion that there were sufficient resources for growth, but they were not getting the growth they needed because of lack of focus, too many projects, and low quality of execution. They realized that they had to construct a growth budget that would be an identifiable, separate section of the traditional budget and that it had to have the same discipline and rigor of review as the cost side of the budget. The division's funding for growth would then be transparent to employees, the CEO and CFO of the corporation, and Wall Street.

The growth budget's explicit approach to planning and funding for revenue growth helps keep the eyes of every employee on what needs to be done to build the business. Making the growth budget a real action plan starts with the following steps:

- Develop a list of the sources of revenue growth and classify them as either short, medium, and long term. For example, let's suppose L'Oreal is trying to grow revenues both this year and on a long-term basis by taking market share from Procter & Gamble's Cover Girl cosmetics line. It could allocate an additional $50 million a year in the growth budget for product development and advertising. A medium-term source of revenue growth for L'Oreal could be to enter into a two- or three-year arrangement with Wal-Mart to gain additional shelf space by introducing products unique to Wal-Mart's campaign to gain market share among Hispanics. L'Oreal and Wal-Mart would work jointly on package design and product features and allocate the necessary funds in the growth budget. A long-term source of revenue growth for L'Oreal could be collaboration with a pharmaceutical company to develop a unique ingredient for skin care that would require FDA approval. If successful, this new product could revolutionize the skin care market and be a long-term source of sustainable revenues, similar to Colgate's success with Total in the toothpaste market.

• Each source of revenue growth and what it would take to make it happen is prioritized and developed into a separate project.

• The costs associated with each project would be spelled out on a quarter-by-quarter basis. If the total cost of the L'Oreal long-term skin care project is $10 million, the growth budget would identify how much would be spent by both cost centers and various business functions, such as on research, product development, trials, FDA approval, marketing, advertising, and the sales force.

• Identifying which people will be assigned to key components of growth projects, what their accountabilities are, and how often they will be reviewed.

WHAT HAPPENS IF YOU DON'T HAVE A GROWTH BUDGET?

We have talked about how a growth budget can help coordinate a company's efforts to increase sales. It can also be a wonderful tool in identifying shortcomings in a company's growth plans. In fact, the shaky foundations of overambitious efforts to increase revenues become apparent when a company lacks a growth budget. For example, recently the CEO of a $12 billion company announced that his firm would double sales within five years. He told the board that half of the growth would be internally generated. The remainder would come from acquisitions.

He was asked what kind of growth budget he had to handle that kind of rapid expansion. He hadn't thought about funding growth in these terms, so he set his team to work collecting all the firm's spending designed to increase revenues—expenditures on such things as product development, sales training, market research, and so on. He found that the number was less than 1 percent of current revenues. (Not surprisingly, he also discovered that the spending for growth was fragmented and not appropriately prioritized.)

Based on his knowledge of what it would take to be successful in his industry, it became obvious to him that 1 percent was insufficient to substantially grow the company. Preparing a growth budget for the first time opened his eyes to the fact that he had to spend more if he had any hope of meeting these revenues within sixty months.

There is no hard-and-fast rule about what a company needs to spend to increase growth. It will vary from industry to industry. For example, in some fields, such as pharmaceuticals, the figure is very high (drug companies will spend between 12 percent and 15 percent on research and development alone) while in others (basic manufacturing) it is substantially less.

But while every industry, and every company within those industries, is different, they all need to have a growth budget and a process for periodic reviews that asks the following questions:

- How realistic is the match between revenue and the costs needed to achieve it? Which costs need to be increased or cut?

- Are the right people being assigned as the project moves into different phases?
- What is the quality of execution and what, if anything, needs to be done to improve it?
- Do any assumptions behind the project, such as market conditions, require rethinking the budget?
- Are rewards tied to the accomplishment of growth goals?

A growth budget is a necessity not only company-wide and in large divisions but in every part of the company that can play a role in growing revenues. Every business unit manager needs a growth budget oriented around specific projects that will be the basis for future growth. Let's take a division of a book-publishing company with sales of $50 million and net profits of $5 million. It publishes books in several categories—general-interest nonfiction such as biographies and history, business, and self-help. Its distribution channels are primarily "bricks and mortar" bookstores, as well as online booksellers such as Amazon.com and Barnes & Noble.com. New books are brought into the company by acquisition editors who use their contacts with literary agents and experts in their respective fields to sign up new authors. The growth budget for the business-unit manager (the publisher) could look something like the following:

- Funds for hiring additional editors to acquire books in new, emerging, "hot" categories.
- Providing editors with enough funding to travel around the world to meet and speak directly with people on the cutting edge of their fields.
- Funds to experiment with offbeat book formats and electronic

publishing in an effort to change the game ahead of the competition.

- Testing new channels of distribution to reach customers.
- For the business-book market, research the sales potential of selling direct to in-house corporate training/education programs.

WHERE DO YOU GET THE FUNDING?

In addition to cost productivity improvements, there are four sources for funding for the growth budget.

First are resources taken away from stagnant or shrinking product lines, with the savings being used to fund growth. Revenue growth was recently made a top priority at Unilever, the global manufacturer and marketer of products such as Dove soap and Lipton tea. When senior management took a serious look at the 1,600 different consumer brands it owned, they found—and this is fairly representative of most packaged-good companies—that they had 400 winners on their hands. These 400 brands had substantial market share, solid margins, and better growth potential. The other 1,200 were basically low growth and using a disproportionate amount of resources. Unilever is in the process of either selling off or shutting down those 1,200 brands and using the hundreds of millions in savings to fund growth of the chosen 400.

Second, take resources from divisions that are either not growing or actually *losing* market share and are destined to continue to do so.

Third is reallocating the money that has already been assigned in the traditional budget funds, such as research and development.

The fourth source of funding comes from a courageous decision by the leader to increase the amount of money he is willing to spend in order to try to gain additional revenues, even if doing so affects short-term financial performance commitments. It takes a brave executive to sacrifice short-term earnings—especially when it is likely to result in disappointing Wall Street—for long-term company growth.

And, speaking of short-term financial performance, what happens to the growth budget when the business faces the danger of falling short of commitments made for revenues and profits? One objection people make when the subject of the importance of the growth budget comes up is that "our CFO will never let us get away with this. He's all about cutting costs, not allocating money for growth."

Actually, the growth budget faces two interrelated risks in every company: demands at times from the CFO for across-the-board cuts and foot dragging or downright disobedience by business unit managers in anticipation of these cuts. Sandbagging happens in many companies, because distrust of the budgeting process is so high. In one case, a division president told her new CEO that she could scrounge around to find $10 million to fund growth for her $3 billion division, but why bother, since, once the money is found, the powerful CFO would take it away.

It's true, of course, that almost all CFOs have been focused on cost management, cash management, and capital budgeting. They need a broader perspective and can, in fact, play a major role in increasing revenues by exercising leadership to ensure the adequacy of funding for the growth budget. And when cuts have to be made—as they invariably do—the CFO can work creatively with the head of the business so that cuts aren't made across the board to growth projects. Some projects should remain intact, others eliminated, and some funded through creative means such as alliances with other firms. A growth budget is an indispensable tool in a company's quest to increase revenues. It shows everyone at a glance just how much the company is spending to achieve growth, and it makes it very easy for the company to support innovative ideas designed to produce new growth ideas, such as "upstream marketing," a subject we will discuss next.

7

Pinpointing Opportunities for Profitable Revenue Growth Through Upstream Marketing

THE CRITICAL FOUNDATION for revenue growth is upstream marketing. It is the ability to create or pinpoint the specific needs of chosen customer segments and satisfy them on a profitable basis better than the competition. Upstream marketing not only helps create profitable revenue growth—it is also a competitive differentiator that creates long-term value for both customer and company.

Most business leaders neither focus on upstream marketing on a regular, consistent basis nor give it the appropriate importance and requisite quality of resources. When people in business think about marketing, it is usually in terms of what I call downstream: brand-building, promotion, and advertising; timely delivery of goods and provision of customer service; and customer relationship management. Obviously, all of these downstream marketing activities are important, but they are dependent on the quality of upstream marketing, where you determine, with granularity, exactly who your customers are and exactly what products and services you can create that will solve their specific needs. Once you figure out who you want to sell to and what you want to sell to them—and it is not as easy as it sounds—then you can start to put in place your downstream marketing program, the advertising, brand-building, and public relations intended to get the customers you have targeted to buy. The downstream marketing program then increases demand.

Jeff Immelt at General Electric, A.G. Lafley at Procter & Gamble, Reuben Mark at Colgate-Palmolive, Dick Harrington at Thomson Corporation, and Andrea Jung at Avon are examples of people who have placed upstream marketing at the center of the behavior of their respective organizations.

There has, for example, been a very perceptible shift at General Electric from the time of Jack Welch, where a major focus was on improved productivity through programs such as Six Sigma and digitization. While chairman and CEO Jeff Immelt is retaining and intensifying this focus, he has made organic growth and bolt-on acquisitions his number-one priority, explicitly putting in place the skills and behavior of upstream marketing in each of the company's businesses. Immelt has programs designed to help GE customers spot new opportunities, figuring correctly that if they grow, GE will as well. The general concept for this customer-centric orientation is "At the Customer, For the Customer" or ACFC. This is not just another slogan for wringing more sales out of customers. Instead, it is a total reorientation of how both the GE sales force and GE technical people interact with a customer to help the customer prosper. It requires the GE technology and sales team to link into the social and decision-making processes of its customers.

GE Plastics, for example, is a major player in an industry undergoing significant structural change. Competition in plastics has intensified, especially low-cost competition from China. There is excess capacity (too many producers facing too few customers) in the industry, and prices are dropping like a rock. GE Plastics has unmatched technology depth and a skill base of converting technology in applications specific to the needs of its individual customers. But if it is going to grow and win against commoditized, cheaper competition, it has to demonstrate how its technology applications add value in terms of the customer's ability to increase market share and improve revenue growth, margins, and cash flow. For example, in the automotive industry, GE Plastics could show a manufacturer like Ford how applications of its technology could reduce the weight of a car, improve gas consumption, reduce cost, or otherwise improve the customer's differentation against its competitors.

GE Plastics has mapped several customer industries where it could get paid a premium for helping customers differentiate themselves from the competition. We'll deal more with market mapping shortly, but GE Plastics is showing that a creative and practical market map and customer-needs segmentation is an important factor in its upstream marketing program for revenue growth. Equally important is building a pricing structure that reflects and supports the positioning of the product in terms of the specific attributes the customer prefers over the competition.

ACFC, like Six Sigma, is becoming part of the GE management philosophy. The strategic, operating, and people reviews of each division are now focused on linking marketing and technology to create new sources of revenue growth and ensuring that there is the right skill mix in marketing, technology, and sales to make ACFC part of the way each GE division does business.

THE MARKET MAP

An important tool in upstream marketing is the market map, which provides a bird's-eye view of the overall market and its different segments. It's a useful way to compare one market segment against another and helps you see the possible relationships between them. The map can also illustrate the positioning of major competitors in each customer segment.

One recent example of effective market mapping was done by the Thomson Corporation, a major information provider to business and professional customers. Thomson CEO Dick Harrington began using the strategy reviews of each of its business units as the foundation for a process of change for profitable revenue growth. Before any discussion of a business unit's strategy or business model, Harrington first

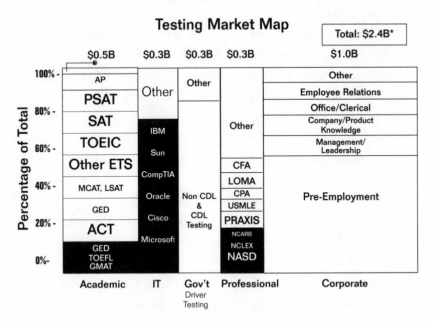

Testing Market Map

Total: $2.4B*

asked each business unit manager to informally describe customers and their needs. Understanding who the customers are and their needs becomes the foundation for making decisions about what the business needs to do.

Thomson's Prometric division provides technology-based assessment and testing services. Mike Brannick, the division president and CEO, in his quest to grow the business, used the market map to provide an overview of the computerized testing market: who the customers for Prometric's products and services are, what their needs are, and why they would prefer Prometric over the competition. Creating a market map does not mean that a company participating in the market will focus on all segments. But it gives a company a relatively easy way to determine whether or not it wants to move into other segments.

Prometric's market map broke the computerized-testing business into five major customer segments: IT testing (e.g., people being certified in the use of products from companies like Microsoft and Oracle to gain or retain a job); government testing (driver's-license certification in the United Kingdom and Ireland); academic testing (administering tests like the SAT, GMAT, and LSAT for the Educational Testing Service); professional testing (license certification in fields like finance and health care); and corporate testing (testing for pre-employment selection of employees).

A large part of Prometric's revenues currently come from the IT, academic, professional, and government markets. The IT market is seen as declining, while the academic market is stable. The big future growth opportunities are seen in the finance and health-care segments of the professional market and in pre-employment testing in the corporate market.

Today, less than 1 percent of Prometric's revenues come from the growing but highly fragmented corporate market. Thomson CEO Dick Harrington and his team see great potential in it for Prometric, and they're placing the tools of upstream marketing at the center of their organization so they can understand the needs of major customers and create attractive value propositions for them.

For example, companies like Wal-Mart, Home Depot, and Lowe's recruit tens of thousands of people a year and have a huge need to reduce the number of employees who experience early termination because of drug usage, theft, or other inappropriate behavior. Many companies do the testing themselves but, since it is outside of the mainstream of their business, are looking to outsource it.

When Prometric goes to a potential customer like one of these large retailers, the tools of upstream marketing help it find and focus on the key decision makers and understand the needs that they have in terms of testing potential employees. Prometric then develops a value proposition that communicates in a dollars-and-cents way how its tests would cut costs, an important issue in a low-margin business like retailing. Of course, the value proposition developed depends on the needs of the customer. A company like Wal-Mart, with a worldwide presence, would have the need for testing in multiple languages and may want to collaborate with an outside firm like Prometric in designing the test itself.

Prometric's market segmentation and mapping also found that pre-employment testing is not limited to relatively lower-level positions in businesses like retailing but extends to the needs of sophisticated financial-services firms like Capital One. Capital One's strategy is based on hiring people with the skills to analyze highly quantitative, disparate credit data about consumers, then using this analysis to discover new customer segments. Once a new segment has been discovered, it designs the right product with the right pricing structure.

For Capital One, the risks in its chosen customer segments are high, but so are the rewards, if the company gets it right. Prometric's value proposition would show companies like Capital One how it can help them select people with the requisite analytical skills that lead to the development and introduction of the right new credit-card offerings.

GETTING UNFILTERED INFORMATION

Upstream marketing is based on knowledge of customer needs. There are easy-to-use tools that can help you gain the necessary insight into what customers want. For example, instead of letting information flow to you through the various filters every business sets up—traditionally, information passes through several hands as it travels from the person who has learned something to the person who can use what has been learned—start by getting unfiltered information from your sales force through "QMI," quick market intelligence. This can be as simple as setting up frequent (say, once a week) phone calls with key members of the sales staff. Earlier, we told the story of Sterling Software and how QMI gathered from the sales force quickly accelerated its growth rate.

As important as timely market information is knowing who is the "customer's customer." In fact, one of your very first questions when doing a customer analysis as part of upstream marketing should be: "Who are our customers?" An example will show why.

Let's say you manufacture office products—pens, paper, pencils, notebooks, and the like—and someone asks you, "Who is your customer?"

The answer most often would be OfficeMax, Staples, Office Depot, and the mom-and-pop office supply stores.

That makes sense. Traditionally, we define a customer as someone who buys from you, and the retailers you named are the ones who purchase your product. You sell to these retailers, and they in turn make your products available to their customers, the people who ultimately use them.

But if you define your customer as just the retailer, distributor, or middleman, you have a problem. The people in the office-supply stores, for example, may be customers, but they are not consumers or end-users. They are intermediaries. They sell the office supplies you manufacture to people who ultimately use them: big companies, small companies, soloists, and even kids who need a pen, poster board, or some highlighters to do their homework.

That means you need to understand every single link in the demand chain.

So, yes, the office-supply store is a customer, but so is the person who ultimately purchases the item. That could be the end-user, but it is equally likely that she could be the head of the purchasing department of a company or an office manager in one of its divisions.

Many companies sell to a middleman of one type or another and don't have direct contact with the end-user, their customer's customer. They consider the middleman their only customer. That is a mistake. You need to understand the needs of *both* the person who buys from you and the end-user, if they are two different people. In our example, marketers would need to understand *both* why the office-supply store does business with your company and why the customer buys your product from the office-supply store you sell to.

Focusing on the needs of your customers—both present and potential—is the starting point for marketing—especially upstream marketing—and the foundation of your efforts for obtaining top-line growth.

Once you know who all your customers are, then you need to learn all you can about their (purchase) decision process, through focus groups, visiting with them, and observing them in action. In the case of our office-supply company, you would literally visit the end-users during a typical day at work so you could see firsthand how they use your products and in what situations. You are trying to discover not only how they use your products but also situations in which they are using something supplied by a competitor and other situations where they are not using what you have to sell but potentially *could*.

Of course, the question to ask at this point is: Do you really have the right people with the right upstream skills who can do all this? Have they been trained to figure out what to look for? And can they communicate effectively what they have learned, so that your company can develop the appropriate products and services?

People who do not have direct contact with customers (especially end-users) are often slow to change their opinions about what they think customers want. You have to convince them, and one way to do that is to actually take them along when you visit with customers.

That is what the marketers at one leading consumer-product company do. They take people from outside the marketing department from, say, information technology, with them as they visit the corporate headquarters and stores of Wal-Mart. The purpose is to see firsthand what people think of their products. Yes, they spend time with Wal-Mart executives, but they also go into the stores so they can observe and talk to the end-users, Wal-Mart's customers. They are looking for usage patterns and regional differences. Are people in certain parts of the country buying more of a product at different times of the year? Are there different purchase patterns among different ethnic groups, or men or women? Do certain consumer segments respond better to different package sizes and designs? The company will examine every variable and take that information with them back to headquarters, where they will work backward to adjust the product—or perhaps come with up a new variation—to meet consumer needs.

The point is that focusing your marketing efforts on the people who are selling your products to consumers is not enough. You have to study the end-user as well and find out how those consumers behave, and how that behavior changes over time. And everyone from the CEO to the people handling customer-service calls needs to have the same marketing focus, if your company is going to grow. You also need to use this information about end-users when marketing to intermediaries.

The skills designed to produce top-line growth require you to understand and define with granularity not only the needs of the customer but how to segment your customers, so that you can capture a profitable share of their wallets.

THE SKILL OF SEGMENTING MARKETS

The underlying premise behind segmentation is this: Every market for a product or service is made up of many different groups. The buyers are not all identical.

All customers are different in their perceptions and their needs. And the perceptions and needs of those individual customers change over time.

Ideally, a company will be able to satisfy each and every one of those customers. However, that is rarely economically feasible. An upstream marketer, using the tools we have talked about, skillfully bunches those individual customers, with their individual needs, into groups that have similar characteristics. Those groups are called segments.

Obviously, if not all buyers of a given product or service are the same, then what follows is that you should be able to position, or segment, what you are selling to each group, in order to increase your revenues.

Let's start with a simple example: to get all the ideas on the table and then move to a more complicated (and representative) situation to show how segmenting, resegmenting, and resegmenting again can be a wonderful tool to help you grow. The key point to remember when segmenting is to choose categories that are reasonably exclusive from one another and then, when appropriate, drill into subsegments.

You might be tempted to say that Cross Pen serves the pen market. And you would be right. So, you could draw Cross's market this way:

All pen users

Everything inside the box would represent potential pen buyers. But this is not particularly helpful. One way to segment the market for its pens is as follows:

DISTRIBUTION CHANNEL

WHY BUY	Department store	Specialty store
Personal gift	GD	GS
Ego satisfaction	ED	ES

(Left vertical label: NEED)

In this representation of the market, there would be four different segments. The box labeled "GD" would be where someone bought a Cross pen at a department store and planned to give it as a personal gift to his son on graduation from college. "GS" would be all those people who went to pen specialty stores to buy Cross pens they would give as gifts. "ED" would represent people who bought the pen for themselves in department stores. And "ES" would be the market of people who went to specialty stores and bought pens for themselves. People buying a pen like this for personal reasons do so for reasons of ego and self-image.

Cross could "resegment"—that is, divide its market in a new way in order to try to gain additional revenue. Cross management, through studying the behavior of customers, could realize that corporate gift-giving was certainly a viable market. And it could then resegment its market to look like this (we won't bother filling in the boxes):

DISTRIBUTION CHANNEL

WHY BUY	Department store	Specialty store	Corporate sales
Personal gift			
Ego satisfaction			
Corporate gift			

N E E D

With the advent of the Internet, Cross could resegment again. Its market segmentation map could now look like this:

WHY BUY	DISTRIBUTION CHANNEL			
	Department store	Specialty store	Corporate sales	Internet
Personal gift				
Ego satisfaction				
Corporate gift				

NEED

There are five key points we can draw from the Cross pen example:

- It illustrates the difference between what a company may think it is selling and what a customer believes he is buying. Cross might think it is selling a physical product, but the customer is buying ego satisfaction, a personal gift, or institutional gift, such as a sales award.

- The allocation of resources and where to focus them for revenue growth become sharper from such a segmentation analysis.

- In each segment, the competition and the attributes of the buyers differ, as do growth rates, price points, and downstream marketing, even though the product is physically the same.

- Understanding the categories of need—why a customer buys—and appropriate sales channels—where the customer goes to satisfy that need—is a critical segmentation skill, gaining in importance as the market, competition, and complexity increase.

- People brainstorming about insights from a segmentation overview, such as the one done for Cross pen, can generate ideas for experimenting with and testing new opportunities.

Every time Cross created a new adjacency—that is, every time it moved its product into a market that was similar to where it was already selling—it had the opportunity to increase revenues.

The segmenting and resegmenting example of Cross can be done by every company everywhere. Let's once again use an example from Thomson Corporation; this time let's examine the division that provides materials to lawyers nationwide, to explain segmenting options in detail.

Just as you could describe Cross as making pens, you could say that Thomson serves the U.S. legal market. But the universe of 800,000 lawyers is just the starting point. In Thomson's case, you can segment the market by type of user (paralegal or lawyer), size of law firm—those with fewer than ten users (paralegals and lawyers), between eleven and fifty users, or more than fifty—and by preferred methods of delivery: online, paper, or both.

You can segment further and/or differently: by region (Northeast, Midwest, etc.), by state, or by type of law (civil, criminal, or regulatory).

Every time Thomson identified a segment—regulatory law, for example—it found not only further segments (municipal, state, federal) but segments *within* the segments (within federal regulatory law, there are lawyers who work for the government and others who are in private practice), and then it drilled down to find *sub*segments (regulatory lawyers who deal with only Equal Employment Opportunity claims) within those segments.

And that was just one way to view the market. Law firms could be divided by usage, and pricing strategies could be designed accordingly. For example, when it came to online usage, some large firms might be willing to pay for all-access all the time, while others would prefer to pay each time they logged on.

The purpose of this segmenting and resegmenting is to find where to put more resources and, also, areas where you could *reduce* your investment.

In Thomson's case, the segmentation confirmed some things that the company had suspected and led directly to the creation of new products. Dividing the market by geography proved management's assumption that a disproportionate amount of business came from a limited number of areas—California, Illinois, New York, Texas, and Washington, D.C.—and that these areas should get even more marketing attention.

But what was more surprising is that when Thomson looked at various practice segments, it found certain specialties—environment, finance and securities, health care, pension and benefits, and telecommunications—in which there was an almost unquenchable demand for information. This led to the creation of specialized journals for these areas.

But segmenting does more than simply discover areas where you need to apply new resources. It can be a way to figure out how you could spend *less*. (In Thomson's case, segmenting customers by usage identified that there were some customers—and some specialized areas of law—that should be served only online, to eliminate printing and distribution costs.)

Since customer needs are constantly changing, segmenting is something that needs to be done on an ongoing basis. As your marketplace undergoes demographic, geographic, or technology changes, look for places to slice up your market in different ways.

When you divide the market into different segments, you can identify an incredible number of potential markets. You can create new adjacencies—the world did not know it needed running shoes until Nike segmented the sneaker market—or you can move into an adjacency occupied by a competitor. Either way, it is an effective tool to grow. The key to segmenting is to truly understand what it is customers want and need. To do that you need to get as close to them as possible, ideally becoming partners with the companies you sell to, offering solutions to the problems that they have. Because this concept is so important, let's spend a bit more time on it and show how it could work in the extreme.

The concept of "being close to the customer" has probably been around for as long as there have been customers and good companies to supply and service them.

But the best companies take the idea one step further and literally (when possible) embed their employees within their customers' organizations. Perhaps the most intriguing part of Jeff Immelt's idea of "at the customer, for the customer." is the one that most people tend to gloss over the first time they hear it. When Immelt talks about "at the customer," he means that the salesperson knows what is happening in the customer's shop. In some cases, the salesperson may actually have an office at the customer's headquarters or plant. The salesperson spends all his time there. He has just the one account.

Now clearly, there are very few companies that can afford to market like this. But the underlying concept is sound, even if you can't have someone in your customer's offices at all times. You want to know everything there is to know about the people you are selling to, and about what is going on inside their organization.

While sticking close to your customers is good, and having senior management call on those customers is better, neither of those moves will get you deeply enmeshed in the inner workings of the customers' business. The principle behind "at the customer, for the customer" is simple: You want to link with the decision makers of the people who buy from you and convert that linkage into greater revenue growth for both you and them.

To become an integral part of your customer's day-to-day business life, you have to be there physically, if the volume makes sense. That's why GE has salespeople inside companies that buy substantial quantities of its plastics; why Colgate and P&G have salespeople with offices within Wal-Mart's corporate headquarters in Arkansas; and why Lear, the world's leading supplier of automotive interiors (seating, electrical, floor, etc.), has salespeople permanently stationed within the offices of Ford.

These salespeople aren't mere order-takers, or glad-handers always happy to pick up the cost of a round of golf or a lunch check. Rather, they are both part of the business *and* social networks of the corporations they sell to. They know where the real power is. They are part of the information flow. They know which of their customers' products are working, which aren't, and where their clients could use some help.

And because they are intimately involved in their clients' day-to-day operations, they can take back what they have learned to their companies, passing on the information so that their firms can use it to create new products.

Now, clearly, there are going to be a limited number of situations in which you can afford to have a salesman at your leading customer's office. If it isn't economically feasible, think of "at the customer, for the customer" being a metaphor for what you are trying to accomplish—having your salespeople permanently entwined in the way your customers do business.

AN UNDERUTILIZED ASSET

Salespeople can be a remarkable source of information and revenue growth because they not only understand their customers but know the inner workings of the companies that employ them, so they can bridge the gap between the two.

There are five questions you need to answer, in order to know whether your salespeople are contributing as much as they can to your company's growth:

1. Do they understand what their customers are looking for from suppliers, and how the purchasing decisions are made?
2. Are they skilled at working with people at several levels, both within their customers' organization and at their own?
3. Are they perceptive enough to see the customers' evolving needs?
4. Once they have gained information about customer needs, how skillful are they at communicating *without distortion* what they have learned so that your organization can act on it, possibly providing customers with new products, new services, a new pricing structure, or whatever else is required?
5. How close is the connection—both socially and business-wise—between those who produce the products and those who provide the intelligence?

The purpose of these questions is to make you learn the extent of the intertwining between your sales force and your customers.

DIGGING DEEPER

Having your sales force deeply enmeshed with your customers' organizations creates a mutually beneficial relationship. What's in it for you is obvious: more business. You become a more valued supplier, with the ancillary benefit being that it becomes harder to replace you, since your firm has become so integral to fulfilling your customers' needs.

But there is clearly a benefit for your customers as well. When used correctly, your sales force becomes another asset for them, another tool that can help them increase revenues.

By spending all this time with your customer, your sales force should be able to not only come up with solutions to their potential problems but should also be able to *help your customers find new opportunities to grow.* Your salespeople should be able to point out to clients markets they have overlooked and, also, be able to suggest new venues for them. (And, of course, if your customers grow, you will too, since they will need you to supply them with additional products and/or services.) As a direct result of you being at the customer, for the customer, those customers should feel that you are supplying them with innovative ideas that will help them succeed against the competition.

Let's use an incredibly simple example to show how this could work. Suppose your firm sells office forms, computer paper, and laser-printer cartridges. A skilled sales force could suggest to their customers—which include the office-supply superstores—that they expand the pond by bunching together their customers through various associations such as AAA, the American Medical Association, the American Bar Association, and the like.

That innovation (on your customer's behalf) will spur demand for what you have to sell—after all, the more of your products that the superstores sell to members of associations, the more money the two of you will make. And that increased business will also tie you more closely to your customers—they are buying the majority if not all of their office supplies from you—making it less likely that they will switch to a competitor.

This is exactly the approach that both Colgate and P&G take in selling to Wal-Mart. By having salespeople in headquarters, they can attend meetings that discuss promotions, discounting, or merchandising. And, of course, it means there is someone who is always on the premises to handle problems should they arise.

But the key reason for them being on-site is so they can look for ways to boost Wal-Mart's revenues.

The idea that you can increase your sales by helping your customers increase theirs has been around almost as long as the thought that you should be close to your customer. But here we are suggesting that you take it a step further by fully integrating your sales force with your customer's organization.

This is one of the most effective things I know in helping your customers increase market share. And helping your customer gain share is one of the best things you can do to grow *your* business.

FINDING OPPORTUNITIES

The last part of this discussion may be the most important: Do you think your people have the upstream marketing skills to create market demand—that is, do they have that uncanny, intuitive capability to identify opportunities?

How can you know?

You can look at their track record, of course. But if the person is new—or it's hard to tell what they have done in the past (because they were part of a team, for example)—there is another way. Simply have them talk to you about their last job and have them describe the various segments they identified in the market, and how they went after them.

You aren't looking to hear about numbers ("revenues went from $6 million to $8 million") so much as about the process they followed in spotting what turned out to be opportunities.

The most critical skill a marketer can have is an uncanny ability to find and define a customer need with enough specificity so that his organization can design products and services to satisfy the customer, making a profit in the process. That is what upstream marketing is about.

Without the skills of upstream marketing, revenue growth becomes more difficult. Leaders frequently delegate the strategic task of upstream marketing to specialists, people who do brand advertising or have extensive public-relations experience. But these people do communications, not customer analysis. As a result, the organization's marketing probably will lack substance.

Marketing is about (a) figuring out what a customer wants, and (b) designing products, services, and programs to give it to them. Your company's marketers need to have both skills.

Once a business has identified that need, it can design products to fill it and, then, communicate to customers what they have come up with.

Most companies—and most people who call themselves marketers—are very good on the back end. They know how to promote the solution and the brand, and they know how to advertise it. But most companies and marketers lack experience on the front end, identifying what customers, and potential customers, want.

That skill is vital, and you have to be intellectually honest and deal with that fact directly. If you have fifty people in your marketing department, you must know with certainty how many can spot and identify customer needs. If your people can't do it, what training is required to teach them this skill?

They need to have it if your organization is going to be able to grow revenues profitably.

8

Cross-Selling: The Art of Creating a Value Proposition

C ROSS-SELLING IS BASED on the idea that you can get a greater share of your customers' wallet by convincing them to do more business with you. It seems like the ultimate no-brainer for profitable revenue growth. On the surface, it's so easy and logical: Get all of your different business units together, bundle products and services, and sell more to customers who have already bought something from you.

And yet the business landscape is littered with the remains of cross-selling initiatives that have failed. The unhappy endings can be as basic as an accounting firm being unable to convince you that it can offer business advice in addition to being able to do your taxes, or as spectacular as the inability of AOL Time Warner (now once again called Time Warner) to sell its Internet customers magazines and books, and its readers on the need for online entertainment. The multiple silos of the merged AOL Time Warner companies patched together bundles of products and services they *thought* the customer wanted, never creating a value proposition that the customer in fact *preferred*.

When you dig into cross-selling failures, you usually find three problems. The first is that the companies never gave consumers a compelling reason to buy additional products from them. Instead of an offering that is seamless, it comes across to the customer as lacking coherence. For the offering to be successful, the customer has to find it not only compelling but better than the alternative of buying separate pieces elsewhere.

The second reason is the failure to identify distinct customer segments appropriate for cross-selling. In fact, one key question for any business undertaking a cross-selling initiative is whether customers *really* want a bundle of products or services from you. If they do, once the right segments are identified, the next step is retailoring offerings so they form a coherent value proposition from the viewpoint of the customer.

The third reason for cross-selling failures is that the sales force of each department focuses on selling its own products. The training of one sales force about the products of another department is insufficient and erratic, and the heart and soul of individual salespeople are rarely captured by the cross-selling initiative. Given the choice of selling what they know to an established customer base, or offering something new to people with whom they have no relationship, the sales force will choose the familiar every time. Despite being given products to cross-sell, the sales force remains part of its original group—the magazine sales force, the Internet division, or whatever.

Their career path doesn't change, so they continue to concentrate on what will get them personally ahead in the organization, and that is, selling the product or products that they have been accustomed to selling.

CREATING THE VALUE PROPOSITION

Central to cross-selling is looking at the total picture of the customer and then working backward to create a value proposition in language that the customer understands. The value proposition is presented to the customer only after you understand his priorities and how his social network of decision making really works. Here's an example of how one company did an excellent job in creating a value proposition.

Atlanta-based NDC Health facilitates the transaction of health-care claims between providers (pharmacies, hospitals, physicians, and pharmaceutical companies) and third-party payers such as insurance companies. It is converting its twenty-two-member sales force from selling individual products, such as claims processing systems, to selling solutions to the big problems facing its customers.

Anyone who has endured a hospital stay knows how complex the health-care system is. Physicians make referrals for patients going to a hospital, and the customer (the patient) usually does not pay the hospital directly. What and how much the hospital gets paid depends on the idiosyncrasies of the patient's insurance plan.

One of NDC's key products has been electronic claims-processing systems that enable hospitals to get paid for services provided to patients. This is a business that has the potential to triple for NDC in two years, given the need in the marketplace. The question that management asked itself was why there was such a mismatch between the potential and actual performance. To find out, NDC had to get close to its customers—and potential customers—to discover what they truly needed from a company like NDC Health. Once it knew, NDC could then shape its value proposition accordingly.

The financial side of running a hospital is an enormous challenge. Questions about patients being ineligible for the services provided by the hospital, doctor referrals being done improperly, and insurance companies refusing to cover procedures are just a few of the problems hospitals face in trying to get paid. The result is that hospitals write off approximately 20 percent of patient bills, and when they do get paid, it takes from forty to one hundred and twenty days to receive their money. The cash crunch problems hospitals face is a *systemic* challenge, especially since the claims process does not have all of the players (doctors, patients, insurance companies, Medicare, and Medicaid) involved as part of an automated electronic claims system.

The business opportunity for NDC is *selling solutions* so that hospitals can reduce write-offs, get paid sooner, and improve their cash flow. For example, how NDC did so with one major hospital group in the New York metropolitan area provides a great deal of insight into the steps necessary to create a value proposition and illustrates an effective cross-selling process.

It took the hospital group, with $4 billion in annual billings, close to one hundred days to get paid. Until recently, the NDC sales representative was primarily selling individual claims processing products with a narrow cost reduction focus to the hospital's director of financial operations. While beneficial, these products did not provide a solution to the hospital's most important and pressing financial problem—its poor cash-flow from the business. That clearly was the way NDC Health needed to position its product. But providing a solution to the hospital's write-off and cash-flow problems meant selling at a higher level to the hospital's CFO and COO and sometimes the CEO. It would require the salesperson to have broader business thinking, enabling him to understand the pressure the hospital is under and the opportunities for NDC to provide a solution.

In the case of the New York hospital group, the value proposition involved reduction in the time required to process claims and cut the lag in receivables from one hundred to eighty days. Within six months of the installation of the NDC offering, the hospital group improved its cash flow by $220 million, an important benefit since positive cash flow in any business is equivalent to blood flow in the body.

All of the value propositions prepared by NDC require substantial input from its various departments, such as legal, pricing, finance, and product development. For cross-selling to be effective, it may mean that, say, the NDC lawyer needs to be involved with his counterpart at the hospital group to eliminate whatever hurdles exist, not just deliver technical legal advice internally at NDC. This kind of positive involvement can be a competitive advantage by cutting the cycle time from initial proposal to closing the deal.

But the critical element in executing the cross-selling process is the salesperson having the breadth and depth of business thinking that enables her to extract the right information from the customer and then use this information to shape a precise, compelling value proposition.

The most effective method for training salespeople in shaping value propositions is the apprentice model used by professions such as investment banking. There, senior partners show inexperienced members of the firm how to work with clients.

Chuck Miller, the COO of NDC, became the personal coach for both sales managers and salespeople as they went about designing a value proposition. He divided the entire sales team into groups of roughly five people each, conducting a daily dialogue by conference call with one of the groups, and did so over a period of several months. Before the call, each member of the group submitted a one-page value proposition for a customer she would be calling on. During the call, Miller discussed each value proposition in terms of specifics and how it could be improved, enabling each member of the group to build her skills through practice.

The process brought to light internal NDC barriers—primarily a lack of alignment between various departments—that were roadblocks in creating value propositions. Through the dialogues with Miller, the sales staff and their managers also discovered patterns of roadblocks among customers and were able to learn from each other in how to overcome them. The process also revealed not only those salespeople who could flourish in the new selling environment but also those who would not meet the new standards.

WHAT THE VALUE PROPOSITION LOOKED LIKE

In developing value propositions, part of Miller's coaching involved developing a template that included the following:

First, getting the total picture of the customer by gathering information that describes his working needs.

XYZ CORPORATION

Value Proposition Account Plan

Description of Customer

The Opportunity

- Relevant information
- Total picture of the customer
- Decision-making unit plus decision-making
  process in the customer's shop

Value Proposition

Customer-Need Definition	**Your Mix of Offerings Uniquely Designed to Customer Needs**	**Your Financials**
• Scope	• Product A	• Your price
• Timing	• Service offering A	• Cost
• Priorities	• Product B	• Capital investment needed
• Nonfinancial but physical terms, e.g., reduce cycle time	• Service offering B	• Profitability inherent in this account
• Psychological needs		
• Customer's business model		

BENEFIT TO THE CUSTOMER

Time horizon	Cost reduction	Margin* improvement	Cash-flow improvement	Revenue improvement	ROI to the customer
0–1 year					
1–2 years					
2–4 years					

*Margin improvement comes from the customer improving his price and/or product mix

137

Then, identifying the customer's key decision makers and their process for coming to a decision.

Third, assembling and shaping the right value proposition, determining the mix and price of offerings and the cost to NDC, and margins it could expect from the offering.

Finally, showing the customer how the value proposition brings quantitative benefits such as cost reduction in the customer's shop, margin improvement, cash-flow improvement, increase in revenues, and increase in market share. Reinforcing these quantitative benefits with qualitative ones, such as increased customer satisfaction and improving brand image, are the crux of the winning value proposition. On page 137 is a template for developing a value proposition account plan.

HOW BANK OF AMERICA DID IT RIGHT

How a large organization can reinvent itself by doing cross-selling and thereby increasing market share and accelerating revenue growth is one of the factors behind the recent success of Bank of America.

In the early 1980s, San Francisco–based Bank of America was the largest bank in the United States. In comparison, NCNB was a small regional bank located in Charlotte, North Carolina. Over a twenty-year period, Bank of America declined and became essentially a California-based regional bank, while NCNB transformed itself through a series of large mergers into a formidable multiregional bank called NationsBank. It merged with Bank of America in 2000. While NCNB assumed total managerial control of the new corporation, it called the new entity Bank of America.

Ken Lewis, the newly appointed CEO of Bank of America, began to integrate operations of the disparate elements of the business, focusing on the customer, cutting costs, and improving sources of revenue growth. One of Lewis's key appointments was Liam McGee. He was named president of consumer banking and given the mandate to build the best consumer franchise in the banking world. One of McGee's major steps was to begin focusing on cross-selling in the fall of 2001.

He first eliminated traditional reporting arrangements. Instead of working for Bank of America of Texas, or California, or any of the other thirteen corporate units, all 48,000 employees who dealt with the consumer market were put into one division. They all suddenly found themselves part of the consumer banking team. By eliminating the traditional regional silos, the move underscored the company-wide commitment to having everyone work together on cross-selling. The entire new division was given extensive cross-training on every consumer product Bank of America offered, with a corresponding change in how they would be compensated. Training was not a one-time event, but ongoing as conditions in the market changed.

In the past, employees "would be a hero for selling one product—such as loans to customers—extremely well. However, it didn't help us to develop a relationship with our customers beyond that one product," says Rodney Ragland, who runs seventy-eight Bank of America banking centers. "We changed that so that you are rewarded for developing a fuller relationship." The company was eliminating the old ways of doing business and highlighting for employees what would be important in the future.

To ensure the new approach to the market would take hold, employees at all levels were given specific goals. Bankers, for example, were told how many mortgages, checking accounts, or car loans they were expected to open or sell each month. At first, these time-based goals were set at low levels. The idea was to build enthusiasm for the new approach. By making sure there were easy wins—singles and doubles—momentum built.

Still, when confronted with these kinds of concrete objectives, there can be a tendency for employees to concentrate on making their numbers, "I have to sell two more home-equity loans today," at the risk of alienating customers with a hard sell. To ensure that didn't happen, Bank of America made it clear that up to 40 percent of an employee's compensation would be based on the customer-satisfaction scores they received.

To give consumers an incentive to switch from niche competitors, Bank of America expanded and tailored its product line. For example, it broadened its mortgage offerings beyond the traditional fifteen-year or thirty-year fixed rates. It therefore gave customers more options and made it easier for customers to do business with them. Today, all transactions can be handled in one place. Before, if you walked into a branch and asked about a mortgage, you were given a toll-free number to call.

And if you do enough business with the bank (a combined $250,000 in deposits and loans), you are assigned a "personal banker" who can answer all your questions and who has the flexibility to match competitors' offerings. But Bank of America's new initiative goes even further.

"We have spent a lot of time developing our value proposition and that has to go beyond pricing," says Percy Simpson, who is chief marketing officer for Bank of America's consumer banking division. "We are delving deeper into specific markets to find out what they want."

Indeed, as Liam McGee adds, segmenting will be the key to trying to get a bigger share of the customer's wallet. For the short term, the bank will be keying on three specific markets: Generation Xers, that is, people in their late twenties and into their early thirties, Hispanics, and mothers with children, in their quest to add one million customers in the next year.

Acquiring more customers in each of these three segments will require Bank of America to change—and perhaps substantially—the way it does business. The bank is still in the midst of learning what people in each of these groups want. "The more we know, the more responsive we can be in offering them additional products," is the way just about every Bank of America manager puts it, but already some things are clear.

Take the Hispanic market, for example. "Many of the customers we will be serving are recent arrivals to America," says McGee. "They often come from places where credit is generally not available and banks are not trustworthy. So, we will have to do a lot of work on financial literacy. And then there are language issues. Do they want to do business with us just in Spanish? If some of them do, we will provide it. When Hispanics represent 60 percent of the growth in our market, I am not sure we have any choice."

To measure how well the cross-selling program is doing, the company put in not only real measurable goals—"We want to open more checking accounts than we close"—but also in systems so it could gain real market intelligence.

"Before, we would celebrate if our assets climbed 3 percent during a year," Mark Reale, Bank of America senior vice president, says, "but what we didn't know was that the market as a whole climbed 6 percent during that time. We were celebrating the fact that we were losing market share. Wal-Mart can tell you what they sold the last hour. We couldn't even tell how well we did last month. That, along with everything else, has changed."

Today, managers get daily results of how well the cross-selling initiatives are working, and when they fall below expectations, senior managers go out and provide coaching. The scores improve, or people are reassigned or let go.

As a result of these new programs, Bank of America is well on its way to receiving double-digit sales growth from its cross-selling initiative. And it is clear that the senior staff has changed the organization's genetic code. You would be hard-pressed to hear anyone in the organization today describe him- or herself as being a "banker." Employees call themselves "retailers" and the description is apt. When you go to Wal-Mart, you usually don't buy one item, you buy several. In the future, Bank of America hopes you will purchase several products (a mortgage, certificate of deposit, home equity line, business loan, etc.) from them, and it is copying the approach traditional retailers take to make that happen.

Taken together, all of the tools we have discussed so far—singles and doubles, differentiating good and bad growth, leadership, revenue productivity, the growth budget, upstream marketing, cross-selling—need to become part of the DNA of everyone in the organization. The glue that holds them together is the social engine, the subject of the next chapter.

9

Creating the Social Engine
of Revenue Growth

IT IS CERTAINLY TRUE that an idea can come to you while you are in the shower, or by having an apple fall on your head while you are sitting under a tree. But the reality is that most ideas are generated when people exchange information. The more frequent that dialogue, the more ideas that result. When those interactions are focused on revenue growth, the outcome is many more singles and doubles, as well as the occasional home run.

That is the underlying idea of the social engine, our term for putting in place a structure that allows information to flow in the right channels throughout the organization.

"So is it just a fancy way of saying that people need to talk to one another?" the skeptic asks.

No. Certainly, communication is part of it, but what we are talking about is information flow, something that is measurable and improvable.

Information flow has these four elements.

1. It is unfiltered. The person who has learned something is communicating it directly.
2. It is timely. They are passing on what they have learned almost immediately after they have learned it.
3. It is simultaneous, not sequential. It goes out to everyone who needs the information at the same time. It is not sent up or down through the ranks, which takes time and, by definition, creates distortion.
4. It is to the point and presented so that people can see how it is relevant to them.

So, you can see that the information is more than just talk. And when it is done on a consistent basis, and done frequently, social relationships form among people, trust develops, and even more and better ideas begin to flow. Architecting the social engine almost always includes unfiltered information from sales and customers. This connection is very crucial. It can even save a company. It certainly did in the case of Jo-Ann Stores.

Disappointing financial results and a future that looked bleak was the not-so-pretty picture that Alan Rosskamm, the chairman and CEO of Jo-Ann Stores, faced in the early 1990s. Cofounded in 1943 by his grandparents, emigrants from Nazi Germany, the Hudson, Ohio–based chain of craft, decorating, and sewing products stores was short of cash. Sales were declining, inventories were rising, and Jo-Ann's store managers were an unhappy lot, because they felt that the merchandise they were getting was not what the customer wanted.

Finger-pointing was rampant not only among the three top executives, but also in departments critical for revenue growth—merchandising (buying), logistics and delivery, store operations, and information technology.

What frequently happens in situations like these is something like the following:

The CEO stands up in front of everyone—or sends a corporate-wide e-mail—and begins: "As you all know, our recent performance has been disappointing. . . ."

From there, he reviews the changes that will be made to improve things: head count has to be reduced, budgets will have to be cut, the CEO will be more hands-on. The speech or memo ends something like this:

> In these tough times, it is imperative that we all work together. Fiefdoms and insularity cannot be tolerated. We must break down the walls. Through collaboration, cross-pollination, and teamwork, we will win.

And then, usually, nothing happens, except for the cuts.

Rosskamm, however, knew that *something* had to happen, and that getting his organization to survive and back on a profitability track would involve more than just talking about teamwork.

The first thing that changed was that he put in place the makings of a social engine. He set up a conference call in order to have a simultaneous dialogue with ten of the leading store managers and Jo-Ann's key buyers and distribution and merchandising managers.

He conducted the call, and the only people allowed to talk were the store managers. Everyone else had to listen and take notes. This first call centered around three critical questions that had been carefully thought through:

- What three items are selling for which we are consistently running out of stock? By the time the third store manager had his say, the answer to the question started to sound familiar.
- What three items are not selling, resulting in too much inventory? In some cases, the product needed to be dropped from the line. But often, it turned out that some of the stores could use the excess inventory of others.
- What is the customer count, that is, how many people are coming into the stores? What percentage of those people bought something? What are the one or two things we can do—without cutting prices—to get more people to buy? Better merchandise and displays? Moving employees around—more people on the floor to help? More cashiers to create shorter lines?
- What is the margin mix? What are our most profitable items to sell? How can we sell more of them? (Again, you can see the linkage between the top and bottom lines.)
- How are our prices versus the competition? Do they need to be lower? Higher?

The first call took place the week before Thanksgiving, and similar calls took place every day for the next three months. Their purpose was not to have people attack each other or for anyone to become defensive, but to collect and sift through relevant information *simultaneously.*

After the call, the department managers prioritized what could and could not be done and made trade-offs and commitments. Responses to issues raised by store managers went out within forty-eight hours of each call. By the time the second week of January rolled around, Jo-Ann had weathered its cash crisis and started to get back on its feet, and has since become the leading crafts retailer in the United States.

Let's be clear about one thing. The point is not the telephone call but the social engine that builds the information flow among the store managers, buyers, distribution and merchandising managers, and senior management. The frequency with which this information flows unfiltered and simultaneously is crucial to profitable growth.

WHY THIS IS SO IMPORTANT

The growth process needs financial resources to develop new products and move into new markets. But it also requires something else: a way of collaborating to transmit ideas, get things done, make decisions, and assess accountability. Obviously, no one would disagree about the importance of collaboration, a topic that gets discussed in organizations as much as revenue growth and cutting costs.

Talking about the need for everyone to work together doesn't do much. Not surprising, the reason there is not true collaboration in many organizations is similar to why growth can be so elusive. There is no clear process to make it happen: no system to communicate progress and no penalties for nonperformance.

If all you do is exhort people to change, they won't. Not only do they need a real, tangible reason to do it—a reason that can be as basic as "if things don't change, you will be out of a job"—they need to know how.

Developing a social engine enables collaboration to occur naturally and helps foster growth.

HOW A SOCIAL ENGINE BUILDS GROWTH

What occurs when people mesh with the efficiency of a pit crew? That's when it is easy to see a social engine in action. Just take a look around the next time you are at the airport and you'll have a terrific opportunity to see what happens when a well-oiled social engine is, or is not, in place. All you have to do is study "'the turnaround" procedures at a given airline.

Here's how a turnaround works. Let's say that plane number 123 is arriving from Denver into O'Hare in Chicago and then heading back to Denver with a new set of passengers. Turnaround time measures how long it takes to get the inbound passengers off the plane, get the plane cleaned and fueled, board the new passengers, and have the plane on its way to Denver. It's the total time from when the plane pulls into the gate until it "pushes back" to head out again.

This process is a great example of a social engine in action, because there are twelve separate airline departments that need to work together to turn the plane around. Everyone from the people cleaning and gassing it, to the baggage handlers and food caterers, to the ticket and boarding agents down at the gate has to work together to make the turnaround possible.

Because of this complexity, it's not surprising that the average turnaround time for most airlines is forty minutes or more. That is not true at Southwest Airlines. It has integrated the daily working of all twelve functions into one social engine, one that the company calls a "turnaround team." As a result, Southwest averages a turnaround time of just eighteen minutes.

How big a difference is saving twenty-two minutes per flight? Huge. It gives Southwest an additional flight per plane per day. That means more revenue from the same plane every day and a lower cost structure. Combining this with a totally differentiated strategy and standardization of aircraft and operating procedures has resulted in Southwest becoming the world's most highly valued airline. Social engines can be a powerful source of profitable revenue growth.

CONVERTING TALK INTO ACTION

The social engine provides the framework for people to work together and communicate effectively to get things done. It provides specificity. Instead of hearing "We need to work together," and then not having a clue about how to do it, the social engine actually aligns the people from different departments and then gives them a defined task to accomplish, so that everyone can work toward a clear, defined goal, such as the way Southwest Airlines's teams turn a plane around.

There is a second benefit as well. As we've seen, every time two or more people work together, a social relationship evolves and spills over into the work they are doing together. Because everyone is clear on what needs to be done, the odds are good that the social interactions will be positive ones. Good social interactions naturally lead to better working relationships and more productive interactions, and that, in turn, makes the social interactions more positive, providing even more fuel for the social engine. As a result, people work together more efficiently, and their individual capacities are expanded. (They are dealing with different people with different points of view.) And because the social engine cuts both across and up and down throughout the organization, the traditional walls between various departments are broken down. That allows communication to occur *simultaneously,* not sequentially. While it doesn't sound like much, it makes a huge difference.

There are two major problems with having the information flow move sequentially through the organizational hierarchy. The first problem is that the information gets distorted. Just like in the old children's game of "telephone," something gets lost every time a message is passed along. In addition, the second (and each subsequent) recipient of the message lacks the context and tone that accompanied what was communicated initially.

The second factor, of course, is the delay that occurs getting the information to the appropriate people.

Even though no one is being malicious, actions one and two result in a lack of trust. That's why simultaneous communication in all directions is at the heart of the social engine.

Now, just like any other kind of power plant, this social engine needs to be precisely built, well maintained, and used correctly. If not, it begins to sputter, as became clear to the management team of a consumer products company I recently worked with.

I asked, "On a scale of one to five, with five being the best, how much feedback is your sales force gathering from customers about (a) what they like and what they don't like about what you sell, and (b) what new products would they love to see?"

Senior management huddled for a minute and came back and said, "Two." The managers said they were to blame for that, at least in part. They acknowledged that they hadn't asked for that kind of feedback.

I then asked, "On the same scale, how good is the sales force in passing along what they have learned to your marketing and R&D departments?"

"One."

In the salesmen's defense, they were so busy trying to solve billing problems and delivery snafus that there wasn't much time to do anything else except try to sell. Still, these scores are indicative of a recipe for no growth. Given the complexity of today's organizations, a crucial role for leaders who want organic growth is to develop and maintain an environment in which collaboration and trust are part of the natural order of things. In other words, they need to establish a social engine.

WHAT THIS IS NOT

Before we show you the effect a well-running social engine can have within your organization, and delve into the details of how to build one, let's spend a minute on what a social engine is not.

The social engine is not a task force. Yes, often different departments come together when a task force is formed, but the interaction is limited to the job at hand (the task) and members of the task force see their work as being in addition to their day job. The social engine, in contrast, is how the organization communicates every day and involves everyone. It is how the organization does business every day.

The second thing to stress is "social engine" is not another way of saying "horizontal communication or collaboration" on an ad hoc basis. Yes, there is communication between people on the same level that takes place within the social engine, but what we are talking about here is far broader.

The social engine traverses the individual silos in the organization. An organization's structure by its very nature hinders collaboration. The social engine encourages it by having (as we will see) everyone in the organization focused on the customer and his needs. By redesigning the organization so that it is outwardly focused—so that it is customer-centric—the traditional organization blockages are reduced. That allows real linkages between various functions (marketing and product development, for example) to take hold. The simultaneous flow of information enables people to align their energies for profitable growth.

HOW DO YOU BUILD A SOCIAL ENGINE?

The process of creating a social engine starts by focusing on the needs of your customers—and potential customers—and then aligns the company's internal workings to satisfy those needs.

In other words, the right design of a social engine enables an organization to become customer-centric.

Being customer-centric is a mind-set. It is a way of doing business where what the customer wants and needs is factored into every single decision that a company makes. These actions are not just based on hunches or gut feel. They are based on specific information gained from the customers about what is important to them and how they make decisions.

That customer-centric mind-set is not complete unless there are linkages between what has been learned from the customer and the departments (sales, marketing, R&D, etc.) that can act on that information and convert it into profitable growth.

These linkages must be your starting point. Then, and only then, can you create the right organizational structure. When you do, you'll discover that being customer-centric has three distinct components. Each must be observable and transparent. Let's start with the most difficult one to achieve.

The hardest part is making sure you are organized by *customer segment.* IBM's sales force is organized by customer industry segments—manufacturing, financial services, human resources, marketing, whatever. Dell is organized the same way. The more you can align your organization to serve customer needs, the better. That's why even if you think you are serving a homogeneous market—such as book publishers producing books for readers—you want to drill a little deeper to identify the specific segment (general-interest reader, people who want information for professional purposes), or by type of distribution—typical bookstore versus online retailer. The more your sales force masters the workings of a particular industry, the better they can serve it.

The second component of being customer-centric? Everyone in the organization—especially the top people—is *constantly talking about customers,* customer needs, and their buying behaviors. Wal-Mart is terrific at this. Customers and customer needs are almost always part of every conversation that Wal-Mart executives have, and are certainly talked about as much—if not more—than cost cutting. (Why is the behavior of the top people so important? Because employees spend a disproportionate amount of their time studying what the boss is doing.)

And the third factor calls for the *customer's voice* to be present at all levels of the organization as often as possible. Is senior management working with customers directly? Are your customer service people feeding back service problems (and suggestions for new products and improvements) that they hear from customers to the departments that can create new products based on what is learned?

These are three central factors necessary to be a truly customer-centric company, one that satisfies a customer's needs.

CREATING THE CUSTOMER-CENTRIC ORGANIZATIONAL STRUCTURE

The major problem, of course, is getting everything in alignment so that you can take care of your customers. The sales force often reports to a different person than the marketing staff, for example. And, to use another example, there may be no natural mechanisms for customer service (or the sales force for that matter) to let the people in marketing or R&D know about what they have learned in talking to customers.

Worse, there probably is no particular incentive for people in customer service or sales, just to pick two examples, to share this kind of information. They don't see it as an integral part of their jobs, since the odds are they are neither compensated nor rewarded for forging these kinds of links.

Clearly, the only person who can create this kind of alignment is the leader—be it the head of the business unit or the CEO of the entire organization.

To do so, he must answer three distinct questions:

- How must our organizational structure be set up so that we earn as much of the customer's wallet as possible?
- Simultaneously, how do we create linkages between the various functions of the business?
- What skills must key managers have to make the customer-centric organization work?

How you answer these three questions will help you create the social engine necessary to power growth.

ANSWERING OUR THREE QUESTIONS

You start creating a social engine by finding answers to our first question: What is the structure we need to earn increased revenue from our customers (or the people we would like to be our customers)?

Again, as you can see, the focus is outside-in. You look at the market need and then line up your resources accordingly.

For example, suppose you are in the coupon business. You print inserts for the Sunday newspapers and for the coupons that people receive from neighborhood merchants. How would you go about creating the necessary organizational structure?

Well, your starting point is the question we raised at the very beginning:

- Who is your customer (and potential customer)?
- What is the need of each of these customer segments?

Obviously, the owner has intuitive answers to these questions. All executives would. But going back to the very beginning inevitably unearths new markets long overlooked or forgotten.

So, the leader of our mythical coupon company would start by looking at the marketing budgets of customer segments: soft drinks, fast food, cereals, toothpaste, diapers, and so on. Next, he would organize his sales force so that they master the needs of each of these segments. He'd then ask what part of their spending is devoted to couponing, or could be devoted to couponing. Clearly, he would want to capture all of their existing coupon spending that he didn't already have, but he would also want to see if he could get them to increase spending on coupons by convincing them his offering was a more effective alternative to what they were currently doing (mass market advertising, for example).

From there he might evaluate what products his firm might want to add to capture more of his customers' business. For example, he could create a "fulfillment" operation to handle the processing and redemption of the coupons his firm offers. (Somebody has to make sure the stores are reimbursed for deducting the coupon's value from the shopper's bill.)

The process would be no different for you. You are trying to establish what you should be selling, or providing, to obtain a larger share of your customer's wallet.

Once you are clear on what you should be selling, you start to tackle the next step in building the social engine—aligning your people against the objective.

Here, you want to ask what is the linkage between your marketing and sales staffs? Is the marketing department really doing marketing? That is another way of asking whether your marketing department is keying in on the people you want to reach (packaged-goods companies in the case of the couponing company), and then determining and creating the necessary programs that will get them to do business with you. Are they doing all of that, or are they just doing advertising?

Then you as the leader want to find out how well all this links with product development. What systems are in place so that the sales, marketing, and service departments can pass along the information they have learned from the customer? Are they routine and consistent?

Your service organization can be an amazing source of ideas that can lead to singles and doubles. They have direct daily contact with customers. If you train your telephone operators to ask a few more questions every time they have an interaction with a customer, you can discover not only what customers don't like about your product offerings—features, or perhaps entire lines that you can eliminate—but also what they would like you to add. That, of course, can lead to the creation of new products, new services, and most important, new revenues.

Gathering this information from customers and potential customers is not difficult. But that information is useless if there is no mechanism in place for those service people to pass along what they have learned to the appropriate parts of your organization.

So, you want your service department to:

1. Ask questions about customer needs during every interaction.
2. Collect information about what they have learned.
3. Transmit that information to the appropriate places within your organization.

If they don't do this, you won't grow the top line as quickly or as efficiently as you should. Growth is extremely difficult without this kind of feedback loop and the proper alignment of your people resources. And the odds are things are not aligned correctly today. The reason for that is simple. Your company, if it is typical, has a top-down organization chart.

To satisfy your customers, you will need to create horizontal flows of information. People who are at the same level in your organization— the heads of marketing, and R&D for example—will need to work together directly.

This may require your managers to learn a different set of skills. Most managers are comfortable in a vertical organizational structure. In this top-down arrangement, they have the power of hierarchy to get things done. They can use their position on the organization chart to control how resources are allocated and how people are paid, and that is frequently enough to get their will carried out.

In the context of horizontal collaborations, managers don't control those levers. They need to persuade people and build relationships to get things done, and this may require skills they don't have. They will need to gain these skills because it is imperative that these horizontal collaborations work.

To create this horizontal alignment often involves dealing with energy-draining, very difficult personality clashes. The heads of marketing and R&D, two people who probably have not spent a lot of time together, may not like each other. It is the leader's job to see that what has to change does change. I will leave it up to you to figure out what needs to be done to have the new horizontal collaboration function effectively. But I stress the collaboration must function effectively. If changes in your organization or people need to occur to make that happen, make the changes.

There need to be systems that have the sales force interacting with R&D on a regular basis and that ensure that your marketing people are getting reports from customer service. And the structure can't be general. You can't say, "Sue, stay in touch with Bob." You need to be specific. You need to say, "The senior VP of marketing will meet with the head of sales every week and review targeted customers. The sales manager must get reports every day on the sales activities of the top twenty-five accounts." You need to have that level of detail. That level of synchronization. When this happens, they are jointly practicing the skills of horizontal collaboration.

The job of the business manager, of the leader, is to create that synchronization. You need to create the mechanisms that lead to the necessary dialogues and interactions. The organization's leadership has to make various people in various departments not only work together, but mesh.

Again, this forces the leader to focus on the operational side of the business. And it usually entails linking marketing and selling to product development and service. If that happens, you will get a larger share of wallet. If you don't have this kind of alignment, if people don't talk to one another, or understand what others are doing, things can't go well. When it comes to the creation of the social engine, the leader's role is very simple. It is all about rolling up your sleeves and getting the necessary parts in place. Then, once they are in place, you must make sure that everything is running smoothly, consistently, and at the appropriate speed.

For example, you can see the impact of effective cross-silo linkages if you take a look at the transformation currently under way at DuPont.

The genetic code of the research-driven firm had always been to go for home runs. The company prided itself, and rightfully so, for coming up with revolutionary discoveries such as nylon and Kevlar. But, as we have seen throughout, home runs are relatively rare. And, indeed, these kinds of breakthroughs at DuPont had fallen off significantly.

Under the direction of chairman and CEO Charles (Chad) O. Holliday Jr., top corporate executives began to wonder whether they could link the priorities of the research department more closely with the needs of customers in the marketplace.

To underscore the new focus, Thomas M. Connelly, a business unit manager, who also has a chemical engineering degree from the University of Cambridge, was named head of R&D. And one of the first things that Connelly did was to change the orientation of the department.

Instead of searching for $500 million ideas, the focus shifted to coming up with innovation that could lead to products with $50 million to $100 million in sales. And to find them, the focus of the R&D department shifted from looking inward—how can we improve the quality of what we have; where will the next big idea come from—to looking outward and trying to solve customer needs, not only through long-term home runs but also singles and doubles.

"Historically, we had invented things and then pushed them out into the market," says executive vice president John C. Hodgson. "But over time, the needs of our customers had changed faster than our ability to keep up with them."

To fix that, DuPont altered the way it allocates resources for R&D. "In the past, we pretty much allocated resources the same way across all of our business," Hodgson says. "Today, the fastest-growing areas get the bulk of what we spend."

To make sure that the resources continue to be allocated effectively, senior leadership is now directly engaged with the top research programs on an ongoing basis.

"Our growth council, which is made up of all the group vice presidents, Tom, and me, gets together about every four to six weeks and reviews progress. We look at the literally hundreds of programs going on across the company and try to understand where we are going to get the most bang for our buck. We treat these high-potential programs differently. We give them more resources and track them more closely. This has brought a very different focus. There is a much tighter linkage between the businss and our research and technology." The executive team's tool for these reviews is an online dashboard that makes transparent whether priority projects are being properly implemented.

As a result of this new focus, DuPont is well on its way to meeting its goal of getting 33 percent of revenues from products that are five years old or less. At the time the decision was made to shift the R&D focus, that number was just 20 percent.

CREATING THE SOCIAL ENGINE: A STEP-BY-STEP GUIDE

How do you do it?

That's a question I am frequently asked when people hear about, and then want to install, a social engine. Consider the following to be your implementation guide:

Step 1. *The top team* realizes that the current ways of trying to generate more profitable revenues are not working well.

Step 2. *They* individually and collectively believe that growth is not only possible, but desirable and necessary. If they don't believe—really believe—that profitable growth is important, nothing is going to happen. If they do believe, the next step is for them to talk to their people and say the company will grow more than it has in the past. The case has to be made with facts. The numbers they put forth must be reachable and believable. There has to be realism and not bravado. For example, senior management might target growing sales faster by 3 percent to 4 percent, on an annualized basis. The number must be large enough to be meaningful, but not so large as to get people to roll their eyes in disbelief. Gaining 3 percent to 4 percent in an environment where everyone else's sales are basically flat is impressive indeed.

Step 3. *The business unit managers get on the same page.* They wholeheartedly endorse the idea of growth and communicate it effectively to their people.

Step 4. *Tools are added.* Everyone masters the growth tools contained in this book and sets out to hit singles and doubles. As the CEO of a $4-billion-in-sales company said recently, "I used to set my sights too high, telling people to search for a half-billion-dollar idea. Working on projects that will gain us another $50 million in sales within three years is just fine. And obviously, if ten of our divisions achieve that, we have that additional $500 million in sales, on top of the growth that would otherwise naturally occur."

Step 5. *Growth ideas are tested.* Each division forms a multi-functional team, operating horizontally, to put the growth engine to the test. They are given one hundred days to come up with a plan that will harvest low-hanging fruit. The one-hundred-day deadline is important because it focuses everyone's attention and forces potential problems to surface quickly. When the team succeeds, it is rewarded lavishly, which, of course, gets other employees to want to participate, and a large number of one-hundred-day projects are launced simultaneously.

Step 6. *Once the short-term wins convince everyone in the organization that growth is possible,* the company starts moving down three tracks simultaneously. One focus is on relatively short-term wins, those that can occur within a year. The second is on projects that can come to fruition in two to five years, and the third is for projects longer than that. The questions that have to be asked are the same: What projects, what budget, what resources do we need? Only the time lines are different.

Step 7. *A monitoring and review system is put into place to make sure that the social engine continues to function seamlessly.* Specifically, the leaders are checking to see that the overall strategy governing the growth engine is the right one, whether the necessary people are in place to execute it and whether the growth budget makes sense. The idea here is to make sure the growth engine is institutionalized within the organization.

KEEPING THE ENGINE UP AND RUNNING

You've created the social engine. The necessary linkages we have talked about are in place. Managers at all levels are talking directly to customers. Everyone is working to identify customer needs and potential areas that can lead to singles and doubles. Are you done? Almost.

You need to do four more things:

You just want to make sure that the linkages will produce good growth, that is, fulfill the four requirements of good growth—growth that is profitable, sustainable, organic, and differentiated. As we have seen, growth alone is not enough.

And you need to start evaluating people against another set of criteria. Not only do you want to measure them against the traditional standards—are they doing their job, meeting deadlines, satisfying external customers, and the like—but you want to make sure that they have three other key skills: they communicate well, they work well as part of a social engine, and they are effective performing in the environment of horizontal collaboration.

Key skills: Communication and information flow

Unless you are digging a ditch on a piece of property you own alone, just about every other kind of work I can think of involves two or more people collaborating. And no two human beings can work together without information flow. Why this is the case is fairly easy to understand, if you think it through. When people work, the primary thing they do is process information, add value, and pass their completed work on to someone else.

But the flow of information is conditioned by relationships among the people handling the information; all things being equal, the better the quality of the communication, the better the result.

How do you improve communication? Ask the following questions (and make the appropriate changes if the answer to one or more of the questions is no). Regarding the people who are interacting:

- Are they clear not only on their own priorities but the priorities of the people they are dealing with?
- If they are working together on a project with a long timeline, do they know what needs to be done during the short term: the next few weeks, next month, the next two quarters?
- Can they identify and eliminate information-flow blockages?
- Are they on the same page when it comes to understanding the processes to be followed to get their work completed efficiently?
- Do they have a mechanism for conflict resolution?
- Do they know how they will deal with people who don't pull their weight?
- Are they committed to helping one another get better?
- Are they recognized and rewarded for horizontal collaboration?

Communication and information flows are central to building an engine that powers growth within your organization, as Jo-Ann Stores learned the hard way.

Key Skill: Getting the Right People

Once the structure is in place, the leader—be he the CEO or head of the business unit—must make sure that he has the right people in place to make sure the social engine runs efficiently.

At the risk of repeating myself, let me again point out this puts the leader deeply inside the operating—and not just the strategic—side of the business. Making sure all this gets done is the leader's job. Execution is something that cannot be delegated.

Because execution is critical, the leader has all kinds of questions to answer as he confronts the issue of staffing:

- Do we have the right people with the right skills for what we are trying to do?
- Are they in the right place?

These questions all flow logically out of focusing on the customer. Once you know what customers want, you then create the organizational structure to give it to them, making sure you have the right people in place to make it happen.

Let's deal with the personnel questions one at a time, starting with, "Do we have the right people to staff what we are trying to do?"

The phrase "right people" has two parts. Employees must have the necessary skills to do the job, of course, but they also must have the right attitude. Not only must they be committed to having the organization grow, they must be committed to the horizontal collaboration that will make that growth possible. Organizational structure, by definition, divides; good people integrate.

If you think about it, the traditional organizational structure impedes collaboration. There are two primary reasons for that. First, people are often stuck in what look like "silos" when you view the organizational chart. They spend their entire careers in finance, or human resources, or wherever, moving higher and higher up within their particular silo and having limited contact with the rest of the organization.

And the hierarchical nature of the organization structure limits collaboration as well. As you have seen, I am a big believer in having senior managers having direct contact with both customers and the sales force. But about half the time when I suggest that to a CEO, for example, he will say, "I can't spend a lot of time with the people in sales. The head of the sales force is three levels down from me on the org chart and he would feel threatened."

Clearly, the way corporations are organized can limit the collaboration that is necessary to produce growth. Only people committed to growth, who understand the importance of the linkages not only throughout the organization, but between the organization and its customers, can produce that growth.

So, this means when you, the leader, are evaluating people, you must do so against three key criteria:

- Do they have the necessary skills?
- Are those skills current?
- Do they have the right attitude?

Let's deal with each of those factors individually.

The necessary skills part is not as self-evident as you might think. Why? Because your people may be defining their role incorrectly. They may have terrific skills when it comes to advertising, but if advertising is all they do, and they are in the position labeled "vice president—marketing," something is wrong.

But even if the person has the right skills, it doesn't mean those skills are up-to-date.

When bottlenecks and troubles occur, it is always easy to rule out someone who has done well in the past when you are looking for the source of the problem. That would be a mistake. The past is past. It is more than likely that the job has changed, and you must evaluate the person against the new criteria for success.

One of my clients told me recently that "our sales force hasn't changed the way they have done things in thirty years." He said it as a point of pride, as a way of giving me an example of how stable his company is and how efficient its processes are. It was another way of boasting, "See how good we are, we haven't needed to change a thing in three decades." But can you imagine how much has changed in the last thirty years and what opportunities they have missed?

Finally, one of the most important resources you have is a match between the dominant characteristics of the job and the dominant characteristics of the person filling it. You are always looking for the natural fit, for the comment, "This person was born to do that job."

Having the right people aligned correctly is a powerful force. Once you do, you have one more question to ask and answer: Do we have the right person to run this particular horizontal collaboration?

Key Skill: Collaboration

Having the right people is a powerful factor in revenue growth. But exactly how, you might wonder, do they work together? Let's take a "typical" meeting to see how the interaction might work, and to show how a social engine has people interacting differently.

If you were a fly on the wall, the first thing you would notice at this meeting is how it is focused. Instead of squabbling about which departments are not cooperating, here, everyone's attention is outside the organization. What do we have to do to get a slightly larger piece of the customer's wallet? This focus jumps out at you, not only because it is shared by everyone, but also because it is in sharp contrast to what happens at the typical meeting. There, the focus is so diluted, it's like watching someone sprinkling the desert with a teaspoon.

As you glance around the room during a meeting, you notice an interesting thing. Only the people who need to be there are there. It isn't a prestigious thing to be present, and the meeting isn't for show. This meeting is designed to get something done.

You can see that by how quickly things move. Decisions are made right there. When the sales manager reports that a third of his people are having problems explaining the company's value proposition in financial terms that make sense to the customer, the CFO volunteers to set up a series of one-hour, once-a-week training meetings that will begin next week. Told that a sale to a major client is once again bogged down because of "incredibly tiny legal issues," the CEO turns to the head of his legal department, who says he will set up a lunch with his counterpart at the major firm for later in the week.

Perhaps what is most impressive about the meeting is what happens in its aftermath. Everything that was decided is instantly known company-wide, thanks to the corporate Intranet, which supplements traditional communication. And all pending matters are followed up on. At the next meeting, the outcome of the first CFO-led training session for the sales force, and the results of the chief legal officer's lunch with his counterpart, will be high up on the agenda.

Leaders at all levels must be willing to make the corporate boundaries porous in order to make horizontal collaboration possible. And that means there is one more question they must add to their checklist when it comes to evaluating employees: "Can they work in a horizontal environment?"

The social engine is the most effective way to coordinate and harness all the power your organization needs to grow. For any set of goals to be achieved, especially revenue growth goals, the right people have to be involved in the dialogue and interactions that will be the foundation for achieving these goals. The social engine is built through practice, with all players working together, making decisions, doing trade-offs, and sharing the same information.

10

Converting Innovation into Revenue Growth

ALL REVENUE GROWTH starts with an idea. The idea could be for a new product or a new service. Or it can be an addition to a product or service that already exists. Or it can be an idea that begins as almost idle speculation—"I wonder what would happen if . . ."

My experience is that employees, from the rawest recruits to crusty veterans of the business, have ideas, and many of them have the potential to help the enterprise. The leadership challenge is to have a social process that helps draw them out. After all, those ideas don't do your company any good if people won't voice them.

The social engine can help, of course. The interactions among the various departments—marketing and R&D, for example, or customer service and sales—will spark more ideas worth pursuing.

Your organization doesn't need to wait for the proverbial lightbulb to go on in order to come up with new ideas. Innovation can be operationalized and that is what we are going to do here: give you a process that you can follow to surface ideas and, then, develop as many growth ideas as possible.

Unlike cost-cutting, growing revenues requires innovation. Many people think only geniuses can innovate. And, indeed, genius is always welcome. But I have found that innovation is a social process and everyone can participate. And, in fact, once the process is firmly integrated into the way the company does business every day, you will find more and more geniuses coming out of the woodwork.

Silicon Valley is filled with geniuses. But if you look at all the successful entrepreneurs who work there, you will discover a curious thing. The vast majority of them worked—often for a long time—at established firms before going off on their own. Part of the attraction, of course, in starting their own companies was the freedom and equity ownership that come along as part of the deal. But another reason for leaving had to do with the fact that their old companies just could not accommodate them and what they wanted to do. Had their former employers handled the social innovation process better, a certain percentage of those entrepreneurs would have stayed and probably contributed in a big way to the growth of their former company.

Let's walk through the process of exactly how you can turn innovation into profitable growth, recognizing that going from idea to launch is never as linear as it appears when you write it down. At each step along the way, I will give you a concrete example of how one division of a company—Honeywell Aerospace, part of Honeywell International—developed and followed a social process and came up with a product that has the potential to increase its revenues significantly.

This was no small thing. Honeywell Aerospace is a leading global provider of integrated avionics, engines, systems, and service solutions for aircraft manufacturers, airlines, business and general aviation, military, space, and airport operations. Like the rest of the company, the $9 billion division, headquartered in Phoenix, Arizona, had been excellent at improving productivity.

When David Cote became the CEO, he wanted to take the company through organic growth, but initial attempts were spotty, primarily due to the fact that people did not feel they had a vested interest in growing revenues.

To turn things around, Cote looked for a division that could model the growth behavior he was looking for. He found a willing volunteer in Bob Johnson, head of the Aerospace division, who was keen to grow Honeywell's largest division.

The graphic below outlines how Honeywell Aerospace moved from concept to product. It's a model your company can use as well.

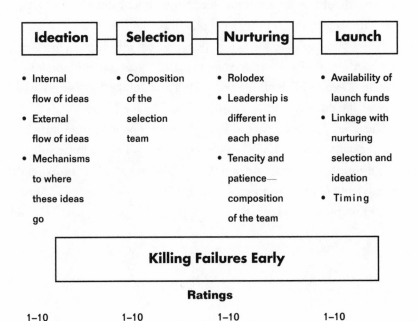

Ideation	**Selection**	**Nurturing**	**Launch**
• Internal flow of ideas	• Composition of the selection team	• Rolodex	• Availability of launch funds
• External flow of ideas		• Leadership is different in each phase	• Linkage with nurturing selection and ideation
• Mechanisms to where these ideas go		• Tenacity and patience— composition of the team	• Timing

Killing Failures Early

Ratings

| 1–10 | 1–10 | 1–10 | 1–10 |

There are five components to innovation—ideation, selection, nurturing, launch, and killing failures early. But before discussing each, there are four factors to note.

First is that all the factors are interrelated, although most people don't stop to realize that. You need to know how all four pieces tie together, because a breakdown in one can affect what happens thereafter. If you can improve the nurturing and launching of ideas, for example, you can improve their flow.

The second factor is that this is an observable process. You can observe and diagnose how well your organization deals with each component. (That is why I suggest you rank your firm's ability to handle each function on a scale of one to ten.) And you will also be able to observe how well your company, or business unit, handles the overall flow within each of these five components. The selection process should be transparent. Everyone should know the criteria that will decide whether the concept will be funded.

Third, you can't pursue every idea, and not all ideas are created equal. After you have surfaced as many ideas as possible, pick the best ones to fund. Kill off the rest. (At the end of the chapter, we will discuss the criteria you use to make that decision.)

The final point: These are five distinct steps to getting an idea into the marketplace. Each requires a unique set of skills.

With all that by way of context, let's discuss the four individual components of the growth process, and show how Honeywell Aerospace put them into action.

IDEATION

Ideation is the flow of ideas that can be converted into growth on a consistent basis. Ideas for new products and/or services can come from two places: inside your organization or outside of it. Let's deal with the internal sources first.

I sometimes hear CEOs saying, "We don't have enough ideas inside our organization. They aren't flowing, and the ones that do surface aren't very good."

Frequently, their explanation for why that is the case is that they have hired the wrong people, or that they are just not creative enough.

That is possible, of course, but I find it is rarely the true explanation.

The reason there may not be enough ideas could be as simple as people not believing that you, the leader, are serious about wanting growth, and so they focus their attention elsewhere. If the leader just talks a good game about growth, but doesn't take action, then people see through him immediately.

Another likelihood: The ideas are there, but they are buried under layers of bureaucracy that keep them from surfacing.

A third possibility: People have potentially good ideas, but they are afraid of raising them, because there is nothing in the corporate culture that will reward them for taking a risk, and many things that will impede their career if the ideas they propose do not work out. That is often a major problem. You need to make sure that employees feel safe taking risks.

A fourth thing to check: How good are the informal networks in your company—say, between sales and R&D—in which people from different departments are constantly talking to one another and fostering ideas? Or are those interactions too time-consuming and cumbersome and employees find themselves cut off from people outside their own department?

The final question to ask is: As a leader, are you *regularly* in your staff meetings trying to come up with new ideas?

Let's suppose you are the senior vice president of marketing. How often do you meet with your head of advertising or public relations and talk about ways you could help grow the business. Is that a dedicated agenda item? How often do you meet with your counterparts in R&D or finance and talk about growth?

On a scale of one to ten, how well are the ideas flowing in your organization? How good are those ideas? Where are they coming from? What is inhibiting them? What will increase their flow?

You, as the leader, are interested in both the number—you are trying to generate as many ideas as possible—and the quality of the new concepts being proposed. Are people trying to come up with only home runs, or are they going for singles and doubles as well? How well does the culture encourage ideas of all kinds? These ideas don't have to come out of R&D. A new idea may involve moving into a different market. Or using a different form of distribution. What matters is a steady flow of ideas, not where they come from.

As for external ideas—that is, ideas for new products or services that are generated outside the organization, from suppliers, customers, and alliance partners—the first question you need to ask is: How strong are the links between the people with outside contacts, your sales force, and your development people? Are they talking to one another all the time, or are there layers inhibiting the flow of ideas? Jeff Immelt's idea of ACFC, "at the customer, for the customer," where you literally become part of your customer's culture, is helpful here.

If you are unhappy with the ideas being generated, check to see that they are flowing in all directions: top-down, bottom-up, and side-to-side. You want to ensure that they are coming from the outside (that is, through interactions with your customers as well). And if enough ideas are not surfacing, identify the root cause and deal with it.

One other thought about this. When an idea surfaces, take a minute or two to help shape it. Help the person who proposes it to take it as far as he can. Make sure it is as fully formed as possible. You want it to appear in the best possible light as it is subjected to your selection process. Doing so enhances people's motivation.

That is what Bob Johnson, head of Honeywell's Aerospace division, did.

"As a division, and as a company in general, we were great at taking costs out and getting things done," Johnson explains. "We were an execution- and productivity-driven culture. But as the economy began to slow down, we knew we would have to come up with ways to grow faster than the economy as a whole, if we wanted to stay ahead of the competition."

The problem was that the people who traditionally succeeded at Honeywell Aerospace did not think in terms of growth, risk-taking, and new ideas. "The company was technical and analytical," Johnson explains. "People were not great risk-takers. We needed to develop creativity and entrepreneurial thinking and take some good risks."

Culture changes like this, obviously, do not happen overnight. But Johnson set out to change Honeywell Aerospace. The company began to recruit and promote people who were creative, and he deliberately fostered an environment in which it was okay to propose new ideas, with no penalty if they were shot down.

At Honeywell, as elsewhere, once people see that new ideas are being taken seriously—and there are no negative consequences associated with the process of proposing them, and indeed are rewarded for doing so—they are more likely to offer some of their own.

SELECTION

You can't pursue every idea. Since every manager at some point will ask you to approve or disapprove an idea, selection skills are something you need to have, whether or not you are in charge of approving large projects. What is your social procedure for selecting the best ideas to give funding? Do you have a mechanism that works? Again, on a scale of one to ten, how good would you say the process is for selecting ideas?

If you give yourself less than a ten, you need to examine the major parts of the selection process: What criteria you require before you approve an idea, who your selectors are, and how they work together. Let's deal first with how the overall selection process works.

It needs to be transparent. Everyone must know that there will be a competition for resources, and only the best idea, or ideas, will be pursued. That means, of course, that the process must be fair and be perceived as such. Politics can't be played, and an idea can't receive funding just because it is the boss's pet project. Anything less, and people will be reluctant to propose new ideas. They won't see the point in participating in a rigged process. Do people in your organization know how the selection process works? How transparent is it?

Once you are convinced that the rules governing the selection process are clear, look at who the selectors are as you set out to improve how your company goes about picking the most promising ideas.

There should be a rigorous screening function for someone to become one of the people who gets to select the ideas your company is going to pursue. If, after he has heard an idea, the first question out of a "selector's" mouth is, "What is the probable return on investment?" he is not the right person for the job. Sure, you want the idea to be profitable, but before asking about potential returns, you need to answer more basic questions such as: Is this a good idea? Does it fit with what we are trying to do? Can we develop it? Is there another way to position it so that it captures an even broader market? These are all questions that need to be asked and answered before you start discussing the potential return on investment.

Yes, you want the idea being proposed to eventually make (a lot of) money. But a positive ROI starting on day one is not mandatory. The growth you are searching for need not be instantly profitable. (But, of course, the longer it is going to take to turn a profit, the greater the return will need to be to offset the initial losses.)

The ROI focus is one of the key reasons that venture-capital-type funding never works within companies. Invariably, the corporate CFO is the key person deciding on intrapreneurship funding, and his focus from day one is—not surprisingly—on the bottom line. (That is one reason you may want to think twice before planning on putting the CFO in charge of the selection process.)

There are four requirements for someone who is going to serve as one of the selectors:

1. **Can she work with the person who proposes the idea and help shape the concept in more than one way, a skill I call reframing?** Often the people proposing the idea don't see in how many different ways it can be expanded or reshaped. The best selectors can shape an idea from different angles.
2. **Can she see the possibilities?** Does she understand how big the idea can become? Can she visualize what success will look

like if it works? Does she understand the implications of success, in terms of beating the competition, expanding into a new market, or whatever?

3. **Does she understand where the idea fits within the company?** This concept has two parts. Clearly she has to understand the corporate portfolio mix, what percentage of sales and earnings come from what type of product, and what, if anything, the company wants to do about changing that mix. (Is one traditional segment of the product line becoming a commodity, and so the company is searching for more proprietary products? Is the firm looking to break into new markets? Into different distribution channels?) Part two deals with how long it will take to get the new idea into the marketplace. At any given point, a company wants a combination of near-term (less than a year), medium-term (two to five years), and long-term products in development so that it can maintain its growth.

4. **Are they willing to bet on the people involved?** No matter how much you develop an idea in the initial stages, there will be unexpected twists and turns on the way to market. When they occur, the people in charge of the launch process need to be able to handle it. How comfortable are the selectors at seeing the potential in the people who will be in charge of the development process?

There are a few things that are implicit in these criteria. We have already discussed the first one. The selector can have a financial background, but clearly her primary focus must be on asking, "What's possible?" as opposed to, "How much are we going to make and how soon?"

The second is that she doesn't spend a lot of time looking in the rearview mirror. The best selectors are not constrained by what has been done in the past. Their focus is not on why something cannot be done—it is on why what has been proposed could be possible. It is in their genetic code to spot opportunities and assume that those opportunities will be successful, until proven otherwise. They pinpoint what will be required in order to turn this idea into a reality. They don't look for reasons why it cannot be done.

Third, she needs to have experience—so that she can see different possibilities. People who are relatively new to the business won't have the necessary background to spot potential problems and opportunities.

What this means, of course, is that you need different types of people, with different skills, experiences, and backgrounds, for each step in the ideation-selection-nurturing-launching process.

Fourth, as we discussed before, the selectors need to be able to balance various time horizons. They need the ability to see potentially successful ideas that could be completed quickly, but they also need to select ideas that have medium and long-term time frames for completion.

Finally, they have to know the difference between ideas that have the potential to be a single or double, and those that can be home runs. Each is important, and each type of idea should be selected and then nurtured. At Honeywell, senior management was cast into this role. "One of the things we did was to meet periodically with the top 250 people in the division, put them in a room, and worked hard to get new ideas out of them," Bob Johnson says. "At the first meeting, we got 465 new ideas. When we sorted through them, combining duplicates and putting like ideas together, we found we had about 100 things worth exploring."

To figure out which ones were worth pursuing further, Honeywell Aerospace subjected each of those ideas to a three-part test. "The first thing we wanted to know was whether it was a strategic fit," Johnson says. "We could make a better ice-cream machine, but it wouldn't fit with what we do here.

"Second, we subjected them to a technology 'fit' screen. We wanted to know if the idea was something we would be good at, given what we traditionally do.

"The last test was financial. This was an attempt to level the playing field. If two ideas were equal, in terms of the first two screens, the question became which one had the potential to give us the highest return."

After subjecting the 100 ideas to the three tests, Honeywell Aerospace winnowed the list down to six, which received a combined $15 million in development funding. Where did that money come from? Johnson had created a growth budget, funded in large part by killing off the division's least profitable ideas.

NURTURING

Once the idea is selected, it needs to be nurtured so that it develops, grows, and ultimately thrives. This requires a unique set of skills; it calls for a blend of creativity, practicality, and social skills. The people in charge of nurturing need patience—things rarely move as quickly as you would like—and they must have the ability to make an emotional investment in people, supporting them as well as their ideas. When people or a team move into uncharted waters, there are always worries: Is the funding going to get cut? Are we going to get taken off the job? Am I going to get fired? What happens if things don't go well?

Things don't always go smoothly, and that is especially true when you are engaged in new ventures. People on the team may need emotional propping up. That is a primary task of the leader in charge of nurturing a new idea. He doesn't need to win every argument. He doesn't have to invent every idea. He doesn't close off dialogue with comments like, "What a stupid idea." He must be nurturing.

There is also a major business requirement. The person in charge of this step in the process must constantly keep reframing the idea from different angles to make sure the organization gets the most out of it.

Here, having the ability to function as a "human Roladex" can prove helpful. The best nurturers are great at knowing who can help develop the proposed idea further. They are constantly flipping through their mental address book to find the names of people— both inside and outside the company—who can help shape and grow the idea. Diversity counts. And so do different perspectives, skills, and mind-sets.

What is the process of nurturing inside your company? How many nurturers do you have? When was the last time they were recognized? If you had to grade your company's nurturing ability on a scale of one to ten, with ten being the best, how good would it be?

If your nurturing rated a three, would increasing it to seven improve the flow of ideas? Yes. A reputation for nurturing invites other people to join your company and encourages existing employees to think more creatively. The more ideas flow, the better the chances that one of them will work. It is another way of building a growth machine.

There are a series of questions you can ask to see how well nurturing works within your company:

• What is the composition of the team that nurtures ideas? As we have seen, they need to have a different mind-set than cost-cutters.

• What is their diversity? Different points of view are especially welcome here, as you try to capture all the different ways the idea can be employed and/or framed.

• What are the social skills of the nurturers? Do they know how to be supportive?

• What new skills are necessary to promote nurturing among the senior managers who will be making decisions about what projects will be pursued and which will be killed?

• What management changes are necessary to make nurturing more effective? Is your business manager a nurturer? How often do you observe him shaping the ideas being proposed? Brainstorming with people? Being supportive?

• Do you recognize that the personality and skills of people who nurture ideas differ from those who conceive and develop them? Are you committed to having different people in each of these roles? (More on this in a minute.)

The answers to all these questions are readily discernible. If you don't see the necessary things happening in your organization, you need to ask why.

Ironically, to be a nurturer you need to be tough. You need a toughness of mind. A toughness of imagination. A toughness that allows you to examine an idea from different angles. A toughness of knowing where the roadblocks are, and a determination to overcome them. What all this toughness boils down to is being tenacious and decisive.

At Honeywell, Bob Johnson took an active role in the nurturing of ideas. He says he found it a welcome change. "Up until now, most of my time had been spent cleaning up messes that resulted from us approving ideas that we shouldn't have. It is extremely enjoyable helping develop something new."

The most promising idea that Johnson helped develop during the first go-round of the ideation-selection-nurture-launch process is a new technology that makes maintaining airplanes far easier and less expensive (details a bit later in the chapter).

THE RIGHT PEOPLE IN THE RIGHT PLACE

Yes, the fourth step in the process—after coming up with ideas, selecting the best ones, and then nurturing them—is the launch. But because the skills are so much different between nurturing and the launching, let's pause a minute here before we get to the final step.

The biggest thing to note is that it is futile to think that the person who came up with the idea and has pursued it until this point will be the right person to run it once the idea is turned into an actual product or service. Yes, in some rare instances, the idea's proposer might be able to do it. But because the sets of skills are so different, it isn't realistic to expect this to be the case. Managers need to go into the process expecting that someone other than the person who came up with the idea will be needed to take it to fruition.

Yes, of course, the person who comes up with the idea may want to run it. And if she feels that passionately about it, you may want to fund her, as she goes off on her own, making sure your organization takes a (significant?) equity stake. But inside the company, you should expect that it will take a completely different set of skills to run a start-up than to create it.

By all means, reward the innovators. Celebrate them. But don't expect them to run what they create. That, most likely, will require a different set of genes.

But do figure out a way to reward these idea-generators. The more you celebrate these people, the more ideas will filter up throughout your organization.

Honeywell Aerospace does that. But the company also does something else. "Before, we would have come up with an idea, roughed out where we wanted to go with it, and then started to act on it," Johnson says. "Now, we ask a different set of questions early on: What could go right? What could go wrong? Do we have the right people involved? How are we going to protect our position once the idea is out in the marketplace? These are all questions we never asked before."

LAUNCH

We have already talked about how the odds are that the person responsible for launching the product/service idea is not the person who thought it up. But when, you might be wondering, should the manager who will be responsible for the launching and profitability of the product get involved in the ideation-selection-nurturing-launch process?

The answer: right after selection. As noted in the chapter on the growth budget, every manager with a profit and loss responsibility needs to review, quarter-by-quarter, the sources and amount of revenue growth and the funding and people necessary to make the launch successful. The growth budget is a commitment process that acts as a lever to encourage the conversion and acceleration of innovation into reality.

Without a serious commitment from the launch manager, through the growth budget, conversion of innovation into reality is like pushing a cart uphill.

In contrast, when the launch manager is fully involved—assigning funds and holding people accountable for revenue growth—it is like pulling a string. Things are so much easier.

But even when management is involved, there are three potential problems you need to anticipate when it comes to the launch process:

1. The launch may come at a time when funds are not available.
2. The marketplace may not be ready for the new idea or service you are about to unveil.
3. Key employees may not be available to help in the launch.

Because these problems can be anticipated, you can eliminate them before they come to the surface through the involvement of the P&L manager.

There are two reasons for this. There is a natural tendency in the latter part of a company's fiscal year, when it appears that a division or company won't make its numbers for the quarter or the year, to start looking around for places to make cuts. Future growth projects are often the first area that gets the ax. Making the manager responsible for the profit and loss of the division sign off on the proposed cuts can eliminate that knee-jerk reaction.

Second, even when broad cuts are necessary, it doesn't mean that everything needs to be cut equally. If the overall goal is to reduce cost by 8 percent, it doesn't mean all projects and initiatives need to be cut by that amount. Again, that is the reason the manager with P&L responsibility needs to be involved. She may know it may be a better idea to keep funding for some growth initiatives intact, while cutting another program by much more than 8 percent to meet the overall corporate initiative.

That takes care of point one. As for the problem that the market may not be ready for the new idea or service, you need to evaluate the risk of investing more in accelerating the creation of the market through advertising and educating potential buyers.

The third point—key employees may not be available when it comes time to launch—is frequently overlooked. Time must be blocked out on their calendars ahead of time. Otherwise, the press of current business could overwhelm their ability to work on new growth projects.

One last thing about this: Once you have decided to launch, create a detailed flow chart explaining what will be done by whom and by when. Then, hold people accountable. This is the easiest way to prevent "slippage."

At Honeywell Aerospace, the best idea to surface from the ideation process is on track. It is the new technology that allows whoever is responsible for maintaining an airplane to scan it electronically for defective wiring and metal cracks. If you picture an X-ray machine for airplanes, you get the idea.

"'Today, you have to disassemble the airplane to do this kind of inspection," Johnson says. "It can easily cost an airline $100,000 each time it is done. Our technology will allow you to do it for substantially less, and perform the work substantially faster."

KILLING FAILURES EARLY

What about ideas that don't make the cut?

The important thing to note here is that if the idea deserves to die—it is not feasible, doesn't fit with what the company is trying to do, won't ever justify its keep, got beaten out by another idea that appeared more promising, or whatever—then it *should* die.

The effect of *not* killing ideas is far more pervasive than people see. The organization's social engine knows who has the power. It knows who is absorbing resources that could be better off elsewhere. There are few things worse than a project that receives continuing support because it is a favorite of someone who has built a political coalition.

Continuing to fund ideas that don't deserve funding hurts everything from idea generation on through to launch. People ask themselves, "What is the point?" if ideas are supported on the basis of something other than merit—and, of course, the selection process. That is why this entire ideation-selection-nurturing-launch process must be objective.

But killing off ideas does more than show people that the selection process is open, honest, and aboveboard. It actually can help the organization achieve profitable growth more easily. There are three reasons why.

1. **It frees up resources.** Money that was going to projects that were doomed is now available for promising projects. And the people who were working on projects that are killed off are free to work on more productive ideas.
2. **It allows people to think more broadly.** Often, when a company is thinking of going down one of two paths, it has people work on both until a clear winner emerges. In those situations, it

is only human nature for people assigned to path A to belittle path B, even if they secretly think it may be the way to go. Once the company decides "A" is not the answer, everyone can look objectively at "B."

3. **It improves judgment.** Obviously, errors will be made on both sides of the coin. Some projects that should have been killed will be launched and vice versa. But through consistent evaluation, you sharpen judgment and set things right.

What is your process for killing ideas that don't make the cut, and freeing up resources that can be used elsewhere? Bob Johnson at Honeywell is relentless when it comes to this.

Not only are new ideas that don't make the cut dismissed, he is constantly examining ongoing projects—using the same three screens we talked about earlier (does it fit; are we good at it; can we make money). The weakest ongoing projects are killed, freeing up not only money, but resources and people to work on more promising ideas.

FOUR MYTHS ABOUT INNOVATION

If you create and follow a rigorous ideation-selection-nurturing-launch process, you will eliminate the four most common excuses people give for why their organization can't grow.

1. **"My business is mature. My portfolio is tired. There is nothing to innovate."** If you follow the template, you will come up with a continuous flow of new ideas and product/service extensions.

2. **"We don't have sufficient ideas."** If that is the situation in your organization, there are two potential sources of the problem. The first is that the internal environment is not conducive to people volunteering new ideas. They think it is pointless—or worse, they believe they will suffer if they propose something new that is not adopted by the organization. The other possibility? People have been looking for only home runs.

3. **"What's the point? They are just going to cut my budget if I show I can come up with new products and services, given my existing level of funding."** Senior managers who cut the budget of people who innovate successfully won't be senior managers for long.

4. **The people who come up with the idea must be the people to launch it.** While it is true that they have a legitimate and vested interest in seeing the idea through to fruition, odds are they won't have the necessary skills.

Conclusion

WHY GROWTH MATTERS TO EVERYONE:
HOW TO TELL IF YOU ARE IN
A GROWTH BUSINESS

Bᴵʟʟ Cᴀʀᴛᴇʀ, the Furniture Globe store manager we introduced in Chapter 1, had a headache as he left work one Saturday and drove across town to attend his twentieth high school reunion. But despite the jackhammer going off inside his skull, he figured he could muddle through. Since about half the people he had gone to school with had stayed in and around town, he would be seeing plenty of familiar old faces, so there wouldn't be any pressure. Besides he was really eager to find out what old friend Susan was up to.

Years ago, they had started together at Furniture Globe, and while Bill had always wanted to run his own store, Susan had always dreamed of being a head buyer somewhere. After a few years at Furniture Globe, she had moved to Kmart, eventually becoming the senior soft-goods (clothes) buyer. She had quit about two years ago—all of the chain's cost-cutting and store closings had taken their toll on her. The last Carter had heard she had taken two steps down the organizational ladder to become one of the buyers of men's clothes for one of the mass merchants who was doing well.

Why such an ambitious person would take a cut in pay and responsibility puzzled Carter. He got his answer when he ran into her by the bar.

"It's simple, Bill," Susan began. "I had to face the fact that retailing was flat, with the exception of Wal-Mart, Target, and where I am now. What I especially like about my new company is that they have figured out how to position themselves against not only Wal-Mart but also Penney's, Sears, and everyone else. Kmart was a mess, and it wasn't going anywhere. And I didn't think Furniture Globe was much better. I really wanted to be part of a growing company—that's why I was willing to take a step back to join these guys. I figured that if the company continued to grow, I'd be back to my old level in no time. It took about eighteen months, and not only am I back where I was, I am actually one promotion ahead. I'm climbing faster and doing it as part of a much better firm. You wouldn't believe the investment they have made in me. My boss told me I'm being groomed for one of the top buying slots at corporate. I can't believe how much I have learned.

"And I can't say enough about the company. The advertising budget is up, every time you turn about they are pushing more and more authority down the ranks, and management actually listens—and acts—when you come up with a good idea."

As Carter listened, he couldn't help but contrast what was going on in Susan's new company with what he was living through at Furniture Globe. She was talking about a company that was vibrant, exciting, and growing. He was living through endless budget cuts, loss of authority, increasing turnover, the end of local advertising and training, declining sales growth, and his overall feeling that his company was in decline. At some point, he stopped listening to Susan entirely and started wondering, "What the hell am I still doing at this company?"

He was jolted back to the present, as Susan paused to take a sip of her club soda and said, "I am sorry I'm talking so much. How are things with you?"

Carter felt he would be disloyal if he actually described what was going on. He changed the subject.

The situations of Bill Carter and Susan illustrate both the business and personal consequences of being part of a business that is growing—or one that is not.

With growth, the organization expands and people can build a career and a future. Growth enables a business to get the best people and retain them. People who see personal growth opportunities have more energy, better morale, and enhanced self-confidence. Growing companies expand into new markets and market segments, new regions, and even new countries. Not only does all that create wonderful opportunities for talented people, but also the growth taps into all the latent psychological energy that is buried inside of employees, and the release of all that previously contained power fuels the organization to even greater growth.

The contrast to a company that isn't growing is stark. First, there is limited room for advancement. Susan could take a step down to join a growing company, convinced—rightly so, as it turned out—that she still would end up climbing further and faster up the corporate ladder at a firm that was increasing the top line and not shrinking. Bill Carter has no such options. Susan is excited to go to work. By contrast, as Bill is learning, it's frustrating to be employed by a company that seems to be going downhill. There is no excitement as you walk through the halls. No emotional energy. Your entire workday is spent feeling as if you are moving underwater.

When there is no growth, a negative psychology permeates the organization. The best people spend a significant part of their time looking for a job, and they leave once they find one. Those that remain make macabre jokes about what form the next round of corporate cost-cutting will take and devote a large part of their days to infighting to make sure that theirs will not be the next head to roll when the cost-cutting ax falls again, as it inevitably will.

If you are not in a growth situation, you are in a limiting situation.

Here are some questions that can help you diagnose whether or not you are part of a growth business. Are you ready to start Monday morning?

1. What percentage of time and emotional energy does the management team routinely devote to revenue growth?
2. Are there just exhortations and talk about growth, or are there actually a lot of meetings and brainstorming sessions about how growth is going to happen? How good is the follow-through?
3. Do managers talk about growth only in terms of home runs? Do they understand the importance of singles and doubles for long-term, sustained organic growth?
4. How much of each management team member's time is devoted to making effective visits with customers? Do they do more than listen and, probe for information and then try to "connect the dots"?
5. Does the management team come in contact with the final user of your product?

6. Are people in the business clear about what the specific future sources of revenue growth will be? Do they know who is accountable?

7. Would you characterize your company or business unit's culture as cost-cutting or growth oriented? If the answer is one or the other, you need to start doing both. Do people in leadership positions have the skill, orientation, and determination to grow revenues?

8. Does the company practice revenue productivity, that is, does it think through whether there are ways to more effectively use current resources to generate higher revenues?

9. How well and how regularly does your sales force—and others in the organization—extract intelligence from customers and other players in the marketplace? How well is this information communicated and acted on by other parts of your organization, such as product development?

10. How good are the upstream marketing skills—that is, the ability to segment markets and identify consumer attributes—in your business?

11. Is the head of marketing in your business an upstream marketing expert?

12. How good is the relationship and information flow between upstream marketing and product development? Between upstream marketing and R&D?

13. Do you have an explicit growth budget in your organization's traditional budget document? How well is the growth budget connected with revenue growth beyond the current fiscal year? Are there funds allocated in the growth budget for medium- and long-term revenue growth?

14. How skilled are the people in your business in creating value propositions for each major customer segment of your business? How effective is your organization in using cross-selling to accelerate revenue growth?

15. How often and how effectively is information shared simultaneously among people who make decisions about resource trade-offs?

16. How good is the flow of ideas in your business?

17. How good is the process of selecting ideas that will be funded as growth projects?

18. How well defined are the steps of the nurturing process in getting revenue growth projects ready for launch? How effective is the process?

Bill Carter ran through these questions on his drive home from the high school reunion. And the answers just confirmed for him what he knew in his gut—Furniture Globe wasn't growing, it was declining.

But although the conclusion wasn't new, this time Carter's reaction to it was. Carter had tasted growth before. As a strong leader, he is used to converting adversity into opportunity. Instead of bemoaning the fate of his company, he drew upon his inner psychological reserves. He suddenly realized that everything we have talked about here is right. Profitable growth can be everyone's business, and it would be his business as well.

As he walked into the kitchen, he was already starting to compile a list of simple things he could do Monday morning that would lead to singles and doubles—steady increases in sales. He determined that he was going to lead and that his whole attitude and presence would be 180 degrees from what it had been in recent weeks.

INDEX

RAM CHARAN is the coauthor of *Execution: The Discipline of Getting Things Done*, the international bestseller that has changed the way managers run their companies. For thirty-five years, he has been a highly sought-after adviser to CEOs and senior executives in companies ranging from startups to the Fortune 500, such as DuPont, General Electric, the Thomson Corporation, Bank of America, Banco Popular, NDC Health, and Colgate-Palmolive.

Dr. Charan earned his doctorate at Harvard Business School and has been on the faculty of that school as well as the Kellogg School of Management at Northwestern University. He has won the Bell Ringer (best teacher) award at GE's famous Crotonville Institute. He won similar awards at Wharton and Northwestern. He was among *BusinessWeek*'s top-ten resources for in-house executive development programs.

Dr. Charan's articles have been published in *Time, Fortune, USA Today, Harvard Business Review,* and *Director's Monthly.* Dr. Charan's other books include *What the CEO Wants You to Know, Boards at Work, The Leadership Pipeline,* and *Every Business Is a Growth Business.* Dr. Charan serves on the corporate boards of Austin Industries and Biogenex. He serves on the Blue Ribbon Commission on Corporate Governance and was elected a Fellow of the National Academy of Human Resources. Dr. Charan is based in Dallas, Texas.